Prime Tennis
Triumph of the Mental Game

Jim Taylor, Ph.D.

Writers Club Press
San Jose New York Lincoln Shanghai

Prime Tennis
Triumph of the Mental Game

Published by Writers Club Press
an imprint of iUniverse.com, Inc.

For information address:
iUniverse.com, Inc.
620 North 48th Street
Suite 201
Lincoln, NE 68504-3467
www.iuniverse.com

Cover design by Gerald Sindell and Jim Taylor, Ph.D.

ISBN: 0-595-09905-X

Printed in the United States of America

Also by Dr. Jim Taylor

Prime Sport
Prime Golf
Prime Ski Racing
The Mental Edge for Skiing
Psychology of Dance
Psychological Approaches to Sports Injury Rehabilitation
Comprehensive Sports Injury Management

To order books by Dr. Jim Taylor or
for information about consultation and workshops contact:

Jim Taylor, Ph.D.
Alpine/Taylor Consulting
P.O. Box 475313 San Francisco, CA 94147
tel: 415.345.9820 fax: 415.345.9830
e-mail: jtphd@alpinetaylor.com
web site: www.alpinetaylor.com

Acknowledgements

Special thanks to Gerald Sindell, my manager, mentor, and friend. His creative and critical input to this book has been essential, and his support, vision, and perspective in my career and life have been invaluable.

I would like to thank the thousands of players and coaches with whom I have worked over the past 15 years. They have been my teachers.

Finally, I would like to express my love and appreciation to my parents, Ceci and Shel Taylor, for instilling in me a passion for maximizing human performance, which has become the focal point of my life's work.

Contents

Preface

When you walk onto the court to play tennis, you will, in fact, be playing two games. The obvious game is the one that occurs on the court against your opponent. The more important game, though, is the mental game that you will play inside your head against yourself. Here is a simple reality: If you don't win the mental game, you won't win the tennis game.

Contrary to what many tennis players may think, at whatever level in which they're playing, the technical and physical aspects of tennis don't usually determine the winner. People who compete at the same level are very similar technically and physically. For example, at the professional level, is Pete Sampras better technically than Andre Agassi? Is Martina Hingis in better physical condition than Lindsay Davenport? In both cases, the answer is clearly no. This is probably true for you and your biggest competitor as well. So, on any given day, what separates a Sampras from an Agassi, a Hingis from a Davenport, or you from your opponent? The answer lies in who wins the mental game. Players who are the most motivated to play their best, who have the greatest confidence in themselves, who play best under pressure, who stay focused on their game, and who keep their emotions under control will most often emerge victorious.

Whenever I talk to serious players, I ask them what aspect of their game seems to have the greatest impact on how they play. Almost unanimously they say the mental part of their tennis. I then ask how much time they put into their mental preparation. Their answer is almost always, little or no time.

Despite its obvious importance, the mental game of tennis is most often neglected, at least until a problem arises. The mistake people make is that they don't treat their mental game the way they treat their physical and technical games. They don't wait to get injured before they do physical conditioning. They don't develop a technical flaw before they work on their technique. Rather, they do physical and technical training to prevent problems from arising. Players should approach the mental game in the same way.

Prime Tennis was created to assist you in just this process, ensuring that mentally you are your best ally rather than your worst enemy. *Prime Tennis* focuses on the essentials of the mental game and shows you how to make your mind work for you instead of against you.

Prime Tennis is not magic dust and will not produce miracles. You would not expect increases in strength by lifting weights a few times or an improvement in technique by working on it for a few hours. The only way to improve any area, whether physical, technical, or mental, is through commitment, hard work, and patience.

Prime Tennis describes issues and problems that are common to tennis players regardless of their ability or experience, and are most likely also important to you. The information, techniques, and exercises in *Prime Tennis* are designed to be "user-friendly;" easy to understand and apply directly to your tennis. My goal is for you to read *Prime Tennis* and go out tomorrow and use it immediately to improve your tennis game.

The information and strategies described in *Prime Tennis* are not really tennis skills or even sport psychology skills. Rather, they are life skills that can be used to enhance any part of your life. *Prime Tennis* can be used in your tennis or any area you choose to improve your performance and achieve your goals.

Prime Tennis has several goals. First, to provide clear and understandable information about winning the mental game of tennis. Second, to offer simple and practical techniques that you can easily use to raise your game to a new level. Finally, to enable you to play at your best tennis consistently.

Using Prime Tennis

There's a great deal of information in *Prime Tennis*. You shouldn't expect to take in and use all of the information the first time you read this book. Winning the mental game is a process that will parallel your own tennis development. It takes time to develop your physical and technical abilities. It will also take time to win the mental game.

Prime Tennis has been specifically designed to make it easy for you to understand and use its information and techniques. It is organized around what I believe to be the most important mental issues that impact tennis. This structure enables you to select the areas most relevant to your tennis. It allows you to find out exactly what you need to know for where you are in your tennis. *Prime Tennis* describes in detail the skills you need to develop for the mental areas that are most important to you. It shows you the exercises you need to practice to win the mental game.

I would suggest the following process in using *Prime Tennis* to its greatest benefit. First, read the book all of the way through. As you read, make note of specific topics that are currently important to you. After reading the entire book, identify the issues that are most important to you and re-read those sections to better familiarize yourself with them. Then, select two or three areas on which you want to work. Experiment with different techniques to develop the areas you've chosen and select the ones you like best. Finally, implement those techniques in your daily schedule.

Now let's begin the exciting journey that culminates in the "triumph of the mental game."

"There are three things you need to be No. 1 and stay No. 1: You need the game, you need the heart, you need the mind."

Pete Sampras

Section I

Introduction

To begin *Prime Tennis*, I would like to introduce you to several key concepts that will act as the foundation for the remainder of this book. One of the most popular phrases used in sport psychology is peak performance, which is typically defined as the highest level of performance an athlete can achieve and it's considered to be the goal toward which all athletes should strive. When I came out of graduate school, peak performance was what I wanted the athletes with whom I worked to achieve.

But as I became more experienced as a psychologist and as a writer, I began to appreciate the power of words and how important it is that the words I use are highly descriptive of what I want to communicate. I decided that peak performances was not descriptive of what I wanted to convey to the players with whom I worked. I saw several problems with peak performance. One difficulty is that players can only maintain a peak for a very short time. Would you be satisfied with playing one great match and a bunch of mediocre ones? Also, once that peak is reached, there is only one way to go, and that is down. And with most peaks, the drop is steep and fast.

So I needed to find a phrase that accurately described what I wanted athletes to achieve. I struggled for several years unable to find such a phrase until one day a meeting of luck and readiness occurred. Walking through the meat section of a grocery store I saw a piece of beef with a sticker that read Prime Cut. I had an "aha" experience. I knew I was on to something. I returned to my office and looked up "prime" in the dictionary. It was defined as "of the highest quality or value." I had finally found the phrase, "Prime Performance," which I believed was highly descriptive of what I wanted athletes to achieve.

I defined Prime Performance, or in this case, Prime Tennis, as "playing at a consistently high level under the most challenging conditions."

There are two key words in this definition. The first key word is, "consistently." I'm not interested if a player can have only one or two great matches. That is not enough to win a tournament. I want players to be able to play at a high level day in and day out, week in and week out, month in and month out. This doesn't mean playing perfectly. Rather, it means playing at a high level with only minimal ups and downs instead of the large swings in performance that are so common among players. The second key word is, "challenging." I'm not impressed if a player can play well under ideal conditions against an easy opponent when they are well-rested and on top of their game. Anyone can do that. What makes the great players successful is their ability to play their best under the worst possible conditions against a tough opponent when they're not on their game. Like the Davis Cup matches that the U.S. has played in South America in recent years: slow courts, dogged opponents, and hostile crowds. Now that's impressive! If the players with whom I worked could attain this level of performance, Prime Tennis, they would be successful.

A question you may ask is, Where does Prime Tennis come from? Though I'll be focusing on its mental contributors, the mind is only one necessary part of Prime Tennis. You must also be at a high level of physical health including being well-conditioned, well-rested, eating a balanced diet, and free from injury and illness. Prime Tennis is also not possible if you're not technically sound. Your technical skills must be well-learned and your tactics must be ingrained. If you're physically, technically, tactically, and mentally prepared, then you will have the ability to achieve Prime Tennis.

Now here is a question for you: Have you ever experienced Prime Tennis? Do you know what it feels like to play at that level? Let me describe some of the common experiences of Prime Tennis. First, playing Prime Tennis is effortless. It's comfortable, easy, and natural. You don't seem to have to try to do anything. Prime Tennis is also automatic. There's little thought. The body does what it knows how to do and there's no mental interference getting in the way. You also experience sharpened senses. You see, hear, and feel everything more acutely than normal. I've heard Andre Agassi say that when his return of serve is on, the ball looks like the size of a grapefruit. At those times, he is experiencing Prime Tennis. Also, time seems to slow down, enabling you to react more quickly. Prime Tennis also has effortless focus. You're totally absorbed in the experience and are focused entirely on the process. You have no distractions or unnecessary thoughts that interfere with your performance. You have boundless energy. Your endurance seems endless and fatigue is simply not an issue. Finally, you experience what I call prime integration. Everything is working together. The physical, technical, tactical, and mental aspects of your game are integrated into one path to Prime Tennis.

"I channeled my mental, physical and emotional energies into my game."

Chris Evert

Philosophy of Prime Tennis

Before you can begin the process of developing Prime Tennis, you need to create a foundation of beliefs about the game of tennis on which you can build your mental skills. This foundation involves your attitudes in three areas. First, your perspective on competition; what you think of it, how you feel about it, and how you approach it. Second, your view of yourself as a competitor; do you play better in practice, matches, or in pressure situations? Third, your attitude toward winning and losing; how you define winning and losing, and whether you know the essential roles that both winning and losing play in becoming the best player you can be. Clarifying your views in these three areas will make it easier to win the mental game and to achieve Prime Tennis.

Prime Tennis Perspective on Competition

Tennis is obviously important to you. You put a great deal of effort in your tennis. Because of this, you put your ego on the line every time you play. When you don't play well, you're disappointed. This may not feel good, but it's natural because it means you care about your tennis.

There is, however, a point at which you can lose perspective and your feelings toward tennis can hurt your game. The key warning signal of this overinvolvement is "too." When players care *too* much, when it is *too* important to them, when they try *too* hard to win, when they press *too* much in critical match situations, then they have lost perspective.

In this "too" situation, your investment in your tennis is so great that it is no longer enjoyable. If you find yourself feeling this way, you should reevaluate what tennis means to you and how it impacts your life and your happiness. You will probably find that it plays too big a role in how you feel about yourself. When this happens, you not only play poorly and lose more often, but you may find that tennis is no longer fun for you.

To play your best and to have fun, you need to keep your tennis in perspective. It may be important to you, but it should not be life or death. What is important is that you have a balanced view of your tennis. Remember why you play; it's fun, you like the exercise, it's a great way to socialize, it feels great to master a sport, and, yes, you like to compete and win. The Prime Tennis view of competition means keeping your tennis in perspective. If you have fun, work hard, enjoy the process of tennis, and do not care too much about winning and losing, you will enjoy the game more, you will play better tennis, and you will win more often as well.

"I have never made sports bigger than life. I just played and enjoyed them. My whole approach was based on what I could learn from sports."

NFL quarterback Rick Mirer

Ups and Downs of Tennis

Another aspect of the Prime Tennis perspective on competition is recognizing and accepting the ups and downs of tennis. In the history of tennis, very few players have had perfect or near-perfect seasons: Rod Laver, Jimmy Connors, Steffi Graf, Martina Hingis. Even the best players have ups and downs. Since they do, then you should expect to have them too. It's not whether you have ups and downs in your game, but how big the ups and downs are and how you respond to them. In fact, *Prime Tennis* is devoted to assisting you in minimizing the ups and downs of tennis.

In a down period, it's easy to get frustrated, angry, and depressed. You can feel really disappointed in how you're playing and can feel helpless to change it. You may want to just give up. But none of these feelings will help you accomplish your important goals: getting out of the down period and returning to a high level of play. This is a skill that separates the great players from the good ones. The best players know how to get back to an up period quickly.

How do they do this? First, they keep the down period in perspective, knowing that it's a natural and expected part of the game. This attitude takes the pressure off them to rush back to a higher level of play and keeps them from getting frustrated, angry, and depressed. It also enables them to stay positive and motivated. Most importantly, they never give up. They keep working hard, no matter how bad it gets. These players look for the cause of their slump and then find a solution. If you maintain this attitude toward the ups and downs of tennis, your down periods won't last as long and you'll more quickly swing back to an up period.

"The mark of true champions is not how they play on the brightest days of summer, but how they perform when things are darkest."

Unknown

Tennis is about Love and Fun

It's easy to lose sight of why you play tennis. There are the trophies, rankings, and attention. Yet, when you get focused on the external benefits of tennis, you may lose sight of the internal reasons why you play. You may not have as much fun and you won't play as well either. When this happens, you need to remind yourself of what tennis is all about. Playing tennis is about two things. First, tennis is about love: love of the sport, love of others, and love of yourself. If you love the game, you have a chance to achieve Prime Tennis.

Second, tennis is about fun. Working hard, improving your game, the joy of competition, and enjoying the process, win or lose, should all be fun. If you always remember that tennis is about love and fun, then you will enjoy the game and you will play your best.

"I must keep my sights on the final goal with more love and passion than the world has ever witnessed. I must let my inner self be out front and free. Love always."

Billie Jean King

Prime Tennis for Winning and Losing

Related to your attitude toward competition is your approach to winning and losing. How you define winning and losing, and your perceptions of the roles that winning and losing play in developing Prime Tennis, will determine your ability to play your best consistently.

Too often, winning and losing are defined narrowly with only one winner and many losers. The player who wins the tournament is the winner and everyone else is a loser. But how many times have you played great tennis, yet lost. The fact is you can't usually control whether you win or lose. What you can control is the effort you put into your game and how well you play. It's fruitless to strive for something that's out of your control, so winning and losing should be defined in terms of things over which you have control. With this in mind, I define winning as giving your best effort and playing to the best of your ability. I define losing as not trying your hardest or playing as well as you can. The nice thing about this definition is that it's within your control, you'll feel less pressure, you'll play better tennis, and as a result, you will probably win more matches.

"It can mess you up if you worry about losing. I'm just going to play the way I want to play. I'm not going to be afraid to lose. If I start worrying about losing, I'll never win."

Andre Agassi

Myth and Reality of Winning and Losing

There are many myths and misconceptions that players hold about winning and losing. Many players believe that the only way to win is to have always won; that winners rarely lose and losers always lose. The reality is that winners lose more often than losers. Losers lose a few times and quit. Winners lose at first, learn from the losses, then begin to win because of what they've learned.

Both winning and losing are essential to becoming a consistent winner. Winning builds confidence and reinforces players' belief that they can play well, meet the challenges of competition, and defeat difficult opponents. There are, however, problems with winning too much and too early. Winning can breed complacency because, if players win all of the time, there's little motivation to improve. Sooner or later though, as players move up the competitive ladder, they'll come up against someone who is just as good or better than them, and since they haven't improved their game, they won't be successful against them. Winning also doesn't identify areas in need of improvement. If players always win, their weaknesses won't become apparent and they won't see the need to work on their game. Winning also doesn't teach players how to constructively handle the inevitable obstacles and setbacks of tennis. Players will be so accustomed to winning that when they finally do lose, it will be a shock to them.

There are also benefits to losing that will ultimately enable players to win more. Losing provides players with information about their progress. It shows players what they're doing well and, more importantly, what they need to improve on. Losing also shows players what doesn't work, which helps them identify what works best. Losing also teaches players how to positively handle adversity.

Rather than becoming discouraged by losing, you should focus on how it will help you become a better player. If you learn the valuable lessons from both winning and losing, you'll gain the perspective toward your tennis that will allow you to achieve Prime Tennis.

"Play tennis without fear of defeat and because it's fun or don't play at all. There is no disgrace in defeat. Champions are born in the labor of defeat."

Bill Tilden

Prime Tennis Competitor

Being the best player you can be takes more than being in great physical condition and being technically skilled. There are many players who have those qualities, but don't perform to the best of their ability, for example, Goran Ivanisevic. Playing your best requires that you have all of the normal things you would expect a great tennis player to have: physically well-conditioned, excellent technique, sound tactics, and the latest equipment. That is not enough though; those things will only make you a good player. You need more to become your best. You need to become a Prime Tennis competitor.

There's a big difference between being able to play well in practice, during matches, and in pressure situations like in the final of a tournament. This difference is what separates players from Prime Tennis competitors. It's difficult enough getting into good physical condition, developing good technical skills, and understanding the tactical aspects of the game. The final challenge is learning how to evolve from a player to a Prime Tennis competitor.

"Some people have a talent for serving and volleying. I have a talent for competing."

Jim Courier

Levels of Competitive Tennis

There are three levels at which you can play tennis. The first level is as a *player*. Players are technically solid and generally play well in training and practice matches, but they don't usually play up to their ability in matches. They perform even worse under pressure. Players typically only win matches in which they are clearly more skilled than their opponents and only last a few rounds in tournaments.

The next level of play is as a *performer*. Performers play adequately in training and practice matches, and perform well in most tournament matches. They can be counted on to win most of their matches and advance deep into a tournament's draw. Performers, however, are rarely able to get that big win that propels them into the semis and finals, and they almost never win tournaments. They don't respond well to the pressures of competition. They're unable to harness the match pressure and raise their game when the match is on the line. Simply put, performers don't play their best when it really counts.

The ultimate level of play is as a Prime Tennis *competitor*. Prime Tennis competitors don't always play well in training and practice matches. They may even occasionally lose early round matches. But what separates Prime Tennis competitors from players and performers is how they respond to pressure. In big matches against tough opponents, their game rises to a new level. Everything that turns negative for players and performers shifts positively for Prime Tennis competitors. They thrive on the pressure of important matches and play their best against the most difficult competition and in the worst conditions. Prime Tennis competitors win the tough matches that propel them to tournament titles and high rankings. Pete Sampras exemplifies the Prime Tennis competitor. He sometimes loses in less important tournaments. When the Grand Slam events arrive though, he wins the tough matches and the big titles. That is what makes him one of the greatest players of all time.

Qualities of a Prime Tennis Competitor

Looking back at the great champions over the past thirty years from Billie Jean King and Rod Laver to Jimmy Connors and Chris Evert to Steffi Graf and Boris Becker, you see in them common qualities that made them champions. Each had unique abilities, styles, and personalities on the court, but all shared several essential characteristics.

At the heart of all Prime Tennis competitors is an unwavering determination to be the best. They are driven to get better and better. They have a great passion for hard work. They spend hours on the court every day to improve their tennis. They love the grind and repetition of hitting ball after ball after ball and they are willing to suffer to succeed. Most basically, their love for hitting tennis balls precedes their love of competing and winning.

Prime Tennis competitors have a deep and enduring belief in themselves. They have the confidence to take risks, to go for seemingly impossible shots, and to never give up no matter what the score. This belief enables them to be inspired rather than discouraged by defeat and allows them to keep faith in their games even when they're missing shots and playing poorly. Difficult conditions and tough opponents are exciting challenges and opportunities to showcase their skills.

Prime Tennis competitors are able to raise their game when they need to in order to win. They seek out and thrive on the pressure of the "big match." They have the ability to stay calm and focused in, for example, the chaos and distraction of a hostile Davis Cup or the pressure of a Wimbledon championship. Most fundamentally, Prime Tennis competitors play their best in the most important matches of their lives.

How to Become a Prime Tennis Competitor

Becoming a Prime Tennis competitor requires that you maximize every aspect of your tennis performance. It starts at the physical level. You must be in the best possible physical condition of which you're capable. Next, you have to develop the technical side of your game. You need to groove your strokes so well, have your technique so well ingrained and automatic, that it holds up when the pressure is on. You must also be tactically skilled, knowing what shots to make and when to make them. So far, though, this will only enable you to become a performer at best. It is the next step that will put you on the path to becoming a Prime Tennis competitor.

You need to be highly motivated to put in the time and effort necessary to be physically, technically, and tactically prepared. You must develop the confidence that you can play your best in the most important match of your life under the most demanding conditions in which you have ever competed. You need to train yourself to seek out and thrive on pressure and have the ability to stay calm and focused when the match is on the line. Lastly, you must have the ability to use your emotions to your advantage so that they help you play your best tennis.

Prime Tennis is devoted to helping you achieve this part of becoming a Prime Tennis competitor. You must be totally prepared for every match: physically, technically, tactically, and mentally ready to play your best tennis. If you can develop yourself in these areas, you will become a Prime Tennis competitor.

Prime Tennis Skills are Skills

Many players have misconceptions about the mental game of tennis. Players often believe that mental abilities are inborn, in other words, players either have them or they don't, and if not, they can't develop them. But mental abilities are skills, just like technical skills, that can be developed. You should approach Prime Tennis skills the same way you approach physical and technical parts of your game. If you work on them, your Prime Tennis skills will improve and your overall game will be raised.

> *"What made me a champion? A mental strength, belief in myself, guts and the ability to never give up."*
>
> Chris Evert

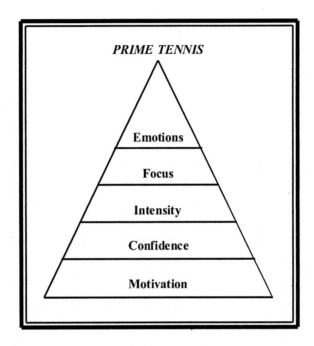

Prime Tennis Pyramid

This book is directed toward helping you experience the feeling and performance of Prime Tennis. This goal is accomplished by ascending the Prime Tennis pyramid, which is comprised of five essential mental factors that impact performance: motivation, confidence, intensity, focus, and emotions (see above). By developing these mental areas, you will achieve Prime Tennis.

These five mental factors are ordered in a way that each area builds on the previous ones leading to Prime Tennis. At the base of the Prime Tennis pyramid lies motivation because without motivation there is no interest or desire to practice. Prime motivation ensures that you put in the necessary time and effort to be totally prepared to play your best tennis. From motivation and preparation comes confidence in your physical, technical, and tactical capabilities, and in your ability to play your best. Prime confidence gives you the desire to compete and the belief that you can win. From confidence comes the ability to manage your intensity and respond positively to the pressures of competition. Prime intensity enables you to consistently maintain your ideal level of intensity so you are physically capable of playing your best. From intensity comes the ability to focus properly during practice and matches. Prime focus lets you stay focused and avoid distractions. From these four mental factors comes the ability to master your emotions. Prime emotions ensure that your emotions help rather than hurt your tennis and that you are your best ally instead of your worst enemy on the court. Having ascended the Prime Tennis pyramid, you will have the tools to achieve Prime Tennis.

Section II

Prime Tennis Assessment

Chapter 1
Prime Tennis Profiling

Now that you have an understanding of Prime Tennis, you can begin the process of achieving it. The first step involves gaining a better understanding of yourself as a tennis player. Self-understanding is so important because it shows you your strengths and areas in need of improvement and enables you to realize how you react in certain situations. This self-understanding then results in more efficient change. Becoming the best player you can is complicated. You probably have a busy life filled with tennis, school, work, family, social life, and other activities. It's difficult to find time to do everything. By understanding yourself, you'll know what you need to work on to be efficient and focused in your efforts.

In developing greater self-understanding, players must recognize their strengths and weaknesses. Most players love to focus on their strengths, but don't like to admit that they have weaknesses. This attitude will limit their development. Most players think that they're as good as their greatest strengths. For example, it's their big forehand that enables them to win. The truth is, however, that players are only as good as their biggest weakness.

Returning to that example, if their opponent keeps hitting to their weak backhand, the forehand is no longer a factor in the match and the poor backhand will determine the outcome of match.

Think of your strengths and weaknesses as a mathematical equation (see Prime Profile Formula below). If you have a big serve (10), but also a poor return of serve (2), your overall tennis performance would be low (10+2=12). If you worked on and improved your return of serve (7), then your overall tennis performance would rise significantly (10+7=17). The more you improve your weaknesses, the higher your overall tennis performance will be and the more you will win.

PRIME PROFILE FORMULA

Strengths + Weaknesses = Overall Tennis Performance

Why Prime Tennis Profiling?

A difficulty with dealing with the mental aspects of tennis is that they're not tangible or easily measured. If you want to learn what are your physical strengths and weaknesses, you can go through a physical testing program that gives you objective data about your physical condition. Think of Prime Tennis profiling as physical testing for the mind. It makes mental issues related to your tennis more concrete. Prime Tennis profiling increases your self-understanding so you can take active steps to maintain your strengths and improve your weaknesses.

It's important for you to have an open mind with Prime Tennis profiling. Rather than being uncomfortable with facing your weaknesses, you should be willing to consider the information in a positive and constructive way. When weaknesses are identified, it doesn't mean that you're incapable of playing well. It may be that you haven't had to use these skills at your current level or you've been able to hide them with strong parts of your game.

"A part of greatness is learning to correct your weaknesses. The first thing is to know your faults and then take on a systematic plan of correcting them."

Babe Ruth

Completing the Prime Tennis Profile

The Prime Tennis profile (see page 23) is comprised of 12 mental, emotional, and competitive factors that impact tennis. To complete the Prime Tennis profile, read the description of each factor and rate yourself on a one to ten scale by drawing a line at that level and shading in the area toward the center of the profile.

Motivation refers to how determined you are to train and compete to achieve your tennis goals. Motivation affects all aspects of your tennis preparation including your desire to put time and energy into physical conditioning, technical and tactical development, and mental preparation. Do you work consistently hard on all aspects of your game or do you give up when you get tired, bored, or frustrated? (1-not at all motivated; 10-very motivated)

Confidence relates to how positive or negative your self-talk and body language are during a match. It includes how well you're able to maintain your confidence during matches, especially difficult ones. Do you stay positive even under pressure and when you're not playing well or do you become negative and get down on yourself? (1-very negative; 10-very positive)

Intensity involves whether your physical intensity helps or hurts your tennis. In pressure situations, are you able to maintain a level of intensity that allows you to play well or do you become too anxious to play well? (1-hurts, anxious or let down; 10-helps, just right)

Focus is concerned with how well you're able to keep your mind on playing your best during a match. It involves avoiding distractions and not losing focus in difficult matches. Are you able to stay focused on what you need to in order to play well or do you become distracted by things that hurt your tennis? (1-distracted; 10-focused)

Emotions involve how well you're able to control your emotions during a match. Particularly in difficult matches or when you're not playing well, do you stay positive and excited or do you get angry, depressed, or frustrated? Simply put, do your emotions help or hurt you during matches? (1-lose control, hurt; 10-have control, help)

Consistency relates to how well you're able to maintain your level of play during a match. Does your level of play stay at a consistently high level or does it go up and down frequently during a match? (1-very inconsistent; 10-very consistent)

Routines involve how much you use routines in your tennis. Do you have a pre-match routine to prepare for a match? Do you have a routine between points of a match? How consistent are you in using routines in your tennis? (1-never; 10-often)

Competitor refers to how well you play in matches as compared to practice. Do you play better, the same, or worse in matches as compared to practice? (1-not as well;. 10-better)

Adversity is concerned with your ability to respond positively to difficulties you're faced with during matches. For example, how do you react when it is windy or your opponent plays a style that you don't like? (1-poorly; 10-well)

Pressure relates to your ability to play your best in difficult match situations such as third sets and tie-breaks. Does your game improve or does it decline when the match is on the line? (1-poorly; 10-well)

Ally involves whether you are your best ally or your worst enemy during a match. Are you positive and encouraging to yourself or do you get

---

PRIME TENNIS PROFILE

Name _____   Date _____

Directions: Twelve mental factors that impact tennis performance are identified in the profile below. Using the definitions provided above, rate yourself on a 1-10 scale for each factor by drawing a line at that level and shading in the area toward the center of profile. A score below a _7_ indicates an area in need of improvement.

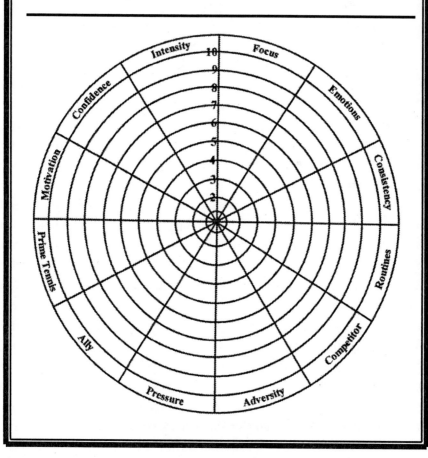

angry and berate yourself, especially when you're behind or not playing well? (1-enemy; 10-ally)

Prime Tennis refers to how often you achieve and maintain your highest level of tennis. Are you able to achieve Prime Tennis regularly or is it a rare occurrence for you? (1-never; 10-often)

Using Your Prime Tennis Profile

Having completed the Prime Tennis profile, you now have a clear picture of what you believe to be the mental strengths and weaknesses in your tennis. Typically, a score below a 7 indicates an area on which you need to work. Place a ✓ next to each factor that you scored as less than a 7. These are the factors that you'll want to consider working on in your Prime Tennis program.

From those checked factors, select three to focus on in the immediate future. It doesn't make sense to deal with every one that you need to strengthen. You'll just become overloaded and won't give adequate attention to any of them. It's best to focus on a few, strengthen them, then move on to others.

The question is, if you have more than three factors on which you need to work, which ones should you choose? The decision should be based on several concerns. First, you should look at which ones are most important for your long-term development. Just like working on your technical game, you should focus on the factors that you will need in the long run. Second, some weaknesses are symptoms of other weaknesses. By dealing with one factor, another one can be relieved without having to work on it directly. For example, you may not handle pressure well because you lack confidence. By building your confidence, you also improve your ability to handle pressure. Third, you need to balance your immediate training and competitive needs with your long-term development. You may have an important tournament coming up for which you need to be ready. For example, you may decide that you need to improve your focus and intensity immediately even though working on your motivation and confidence will be more important in the future.

Using the Prime Tennis Priority form (see page 26), indicate the three mental factors you want to focus on in the near future. After reading *Prime Tennis*, return to the relevant chapters to learn about techniques and exercises that will help you strengthen the areas you've selected. Use the goal setting and Prime Tennis program described in Section V to work on those areas.

You can also use Prime Tennis Profiling to measure progress in your training. Periodically, perhaps once a month, complete the profile and compare it with your past profiles. You should see improvement in the areas on which you've worked. Also, ask your coaches about positive changes they've seen in those areas. When your ratings move above 7, select other factors to work on and follow the same procedure.

"World-class tennis is 60 percent mental. There is very little difference in the stroke capabilities of the top players."

Pat Cash

PRIME TENNIS PRIORITY

Name _____   **Date** _____

Directions: In the space below, indicate three areas that you have identified in your Prime Tennis profile on which you would like to focus in your tennis. As these areas improve and new areas need work, complete this form again to specify the new priorities.

1.

2.

3.

Chapter 2

Playing Styles

One of the beauties of tennis is appreciating the diverse styles that players have. It is as much a pleasure to watch Pete Sampras as it is Andre Agassi or Lindsay Davenport as it is Jana Novotna, even though they have vastly different playing styles. When I speak of playing styles, I am not referring to precisely how they hit the ball or how they look technically. Rather, I am speaking of the overall tactical approach they take to the game.

Several contributors determine what kind of playing style someone develops. Playing style is based your physical attributes and capabilities. If players are tall and have good hands, then they may have evolved into serve and volleyers, for example, Greg Rusedski. If they're short and quick, a baseline game probably developed, for instance, Michael Chang.

Playing styles should also emerge from an understanding of technical strengths and weaknesses. If players hit their groundstrokes with power, then they probably play an aggressive baseline game like Venus Williams. If they have a weak backhand, they might have learned to shade themselves toward the ad court so most of their groundstrokes are forehands such as Steffi Graf.

The final contributor to playing style is personality. Players should play a game that is consistent with their basic nature as a person. If they're naturally asssertive and like to be in control, a power game could be appropriate like Serena Williams. If they're more more even-tempered and patient, they may develop into a counterpuncher such as Arantxa Sanchez-Vicario.

This last influence has become more apparent and important to me in recent years as I have worked with players in which their playing styles were in conflict with their personalities. One highly-ranked junior player I worked with illustrated this inconsistency well. She was an outgoing, energetic, and impatient girl who was always on the move. She was also an exceptional athlete with good speed and great hand-eye coordination. Her new coach was, in contrast, an easy-going fellow who played a back-court game. He made the mistake of teaching her a playing style based on who he was rather than who she was.

After several months in which she endured several losses to players that she had previously defeated, it became clear that this playing style was not working for her. In fact, this strategy was doomed to fail because her personality would not allow her to play such a patient and deliberate style of tennis. When they realized this, they switched her to an all-court game that was more suited to her personality based on attacking groundstrokes and looking for a short ball in which to approach the net and put away a volley. This match between her personality and her playing style proved to be successful and her game and rankings improved dramatically.

Whether you know it or not, you too have a particular playing style. In order for you to achieve Prime Tennis, you must be sure that your style is consistent with your physical, technical, and mental capabilities. To do otherwise would be to guarantee that you would never play the best tennis of which you are capable because your playing style would conflict with essential aspects of who you are and how you are capable of playing.

Playing Styles

There are four fundamental playing styles in tennis. Each relies on different physical, technical, and mental assets to maximize a player's abilities. Keep in mind that physical and technical capabilities, and personality styles are not absolutely related to playing styles. Playing style can evolve for many reasons unrelated to these three areas such as the generation in which players picked up tennis, from whom they learned the game, the surface they played on most often, and just chance. As I describe the playing styles, you should identify which style most resembles your game. Also, get a sense of whether your playing style is consistent with your physical, technical, and mental strengths.

Counterpuncher. The strength of counterpunchers, also known as the human backboard, is their ability to run down balls and get them back. Consistency is their greatest asset. Arantxa Sanchez-Vicario and Michael Chang exemplify this style. Neither have noticeable strengths in their groundstrokes or serves. Their greatest attributes are their foot speed (to run balls down), their consistency (they make their opponents win the point), and their patience (they're willing to stay out there for as long as it takes).

Effective counterpunchers tend to be shorter in stature, slighter of build, and very good at moving laterally. They have reliable groundstrokes that have no glaring weaknesses that would cause them to "lose" their stroke. Their serve generally lacks power, but relies on spin and placement to keep their opponents off guard. They get a high percentage of first serves in. Their match statistics indicate few winners, but also few unforced errors.

Counterpunchers are highly motivated players. This determination allows them to grind out points and maintain their determination during a long match. They are confident in their playing style and generally handle pressure situations well. They're able to maintain effective focus for extended periods. Counterpunchers don't get flustered easily or experience overintensity because they know that their consistent game will stand up to the pressure. Counterpunchers are usually even-keeled emotionally. They get neither too excited when they're playing well nor too upset when they make errors. Counterpunchers are patient and methodical players.

Attacking baseliner. The attacking baseliner's playing style is built around a big groundstroke weapon, usually the forehand. Serena Williams and Andre Agassi are examples of the attacking baseliner. They hit with pace off both sides and have the consistency to grind out points before hitting a winner. Their strength is their ability to set up points with the use of pace, depth, and angles, put their opponent on the defensive, and, when a weak ball presents itself, to hit a winner or cause a forced error.

Attacking baseliners are typically bigger and stronger than counterpunchers. They move well around the court which allows them to set up a point effectively before using their big shot to end the point. Their groundstrokes are generally consistent, but because they go for their shots more, their strokes can desert them at times. Attacking baseliners often have either a fairly big serve (like Serena Williams) or a good return of serve (like Andre Agassi). Their match statistics reflect a large number of winners, but also quite a few unforced errors (especially if they're not on their game).

Attacking baseliners are assertive, but not necessarily aggressive players. They like being in control. Knowing that they have a big weapon gives them the confidence that they can dominate. But their confidence can be fragile if, for some reason, they are not on their game. They can be hot or cold when the pressure is on. If their game is not clicking, they can lose focus and become anxious, which hurts their game more. Attacking baseliners are generally contained emotionally, but become fired up when they're playing well in, for example, a third-set tiebreak, or upset when they're playing poorly.

All-court player. The playing style of the all-court player is built around balance and a strong overall game. Yevgeny Kafelnikov and Martina Hingis are two of the best all-court players in the game today. All-court players do most things on the court well. Their strength lies in their versatility and their ability to adapt their game to the style of their opponent and the needs of the match situation.

All-court players are often bigger and stronger than attacking baseliners. They are not as quick afoot, but their size enables them to hit with power and to move quickly to the net and volley with authority. They have no exceptional technical strengths nor do they have any glaring weaknesses. All-court players typically have strong serves behind which they can serve and volley. They can stay back and grind out points, they can hit winners from the backcourt, and they can come to the net and put away a volley with equal adeptness.

All-court players have a mixture of personality qualities. They must be motivated and patient to set up points. At the same time, they must be assertive enough to jump on a weak return and aggressive enough to rush the net on a short ball. All-court players' confidence is usually quite high because they know they have a lot of "tools in their toolbox." If one part of their game is not working, they know they can turn to another style that may be more effective. This versatility also serves them well in pressure situations because they have many ways to approach the point. There is no clear emotional style among all-court players. However, if you look at Kafelnikov and Hingis, you see two players who are relatively contained and in control emotionally when they're winning, but who can completely lose emotional control when they're losing.

Serve-and-volley player. Serve-and-volley players' games are self-evident; their strength lies in their ability to come to the net behind a serve and volley to end the point quickly. Richard Krajcek and Jana Novotna are two pros who play serve-and-volley games. Serve and volley players have big serves and look for every opportunity to come to the net as soon as possible. Their goal is to overpower their opponents into submission.

Serve-and-volley players are some of the biggest and strongest players in the game. Their size and strength allow them to hit big serves, approach the net in a few long strides, and to cover the net and reach potential passing shots hit by their opponents. They possess a powerful first serve that, when on, gives them many free points in the form of aces and service winners. They usually have a strong second serve that relies on spin, placement, and depth which also allows them come to the net on second serves as well. Their groundstrokes are usually not very strong and they are at their worst in long baseline rallies.

Serve-and-volley players have an aggressive mindset in their game, but are not necessarily aggressive by nature. For example, Krajcek and Novotna (and Sampras, for that matter) are gentle and quiet people off the court. However, on-court, their playing style is one of aggressiveness, relentless attack, and domination through power and intimidation. They have confidence that their firepower will discourage opponents and cause them surrender under the persistent pressure of their big serve and their ever-presence at the net. Serve-and-volley players typically are emotionally contained and direct their emotions into the power of their serve and the authority of their volleys.

What is Your Playing Style?

You want to determine what is your playing style and whether there is some consistency between your playing style and your physical, technical, and mental strengths. Unless you're a player who had your playing style built deliberately around your strengths (most top juniors and pros do this), there may not be total alignment between the three areas and your playing style. If one or two of the three areas match up, that's great. If they don't match up at all, this doesn't mean that you need to completely change your playing style. It may be that you've developed an effective game regardless.

At the same time, you might experiment with a playing style that better fits your physical, technical, and mental abilities and see how you play and how you feel. Use the Playing Style Identification form (see page 34) to identify your physical, technical, and mental assets, your current playing style, and, if there is some inconsistency, what your ideal playing style might be.

PLAYING STYLE INDENTIFICATION

Directions: In the space below, identify your current playing style by placing an **X** in the appropriate box. Then, describe your physical, technical, and mental strengths. Next, specify whether your current playing style is consistent with your physical, technical, and mental assets by circling the appropriate choice. Finally, indicate what is your ideal playing style.

☐

Counterpuncher

☐

Aggressive Baseliner

☐

All-Court

☐

Serve and Volley

Physical   **Technical**   **Mental**

Consistent   **Inconsistent**

Ideal Playing Style _____

Section III

Prime Tennis Pyramid

Chapter 3
Motivation

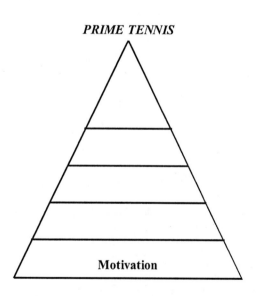

PRIME TENNIS

Motivation

Motivation lies at the base of the Prime Tennis pyramid. Without players' desire and determination to improve their tennis, all of the other mental factors, confidence, intensity, focus, and emotions, are meaningless. To become the best tennis player they can be, they must be motivated to do what it takes to maximize their ability.

Motivation, simply defined, is the ability to initiate and persist at a task. To play their best, players must want to begin the process of developing as a player and they must be willing to maintain their efforts until they have achieved their goals. Motivation in tennis is so important because players must be willing to work hard in the face of fatigue, boredom, pain, and the desire to do other things. Motivation will impact everything that influences tennis: physical conditioning, technical and tactical training, mental preparation, and general lifestyle including sleep, diet, school or work, and relationships.

The reason motivation is so important is that it is the only contributor to tennis performance over which players have control. My Performance Formula (see below) helps explain this notion. There are three things that affect how well players play. First, their ability, which includes their physical, technical, tactical, and mental capabilities, impacts their level of play. Though these four factors can change over time with practice, on any given day, players can not alter them dramatically. For example, a player is not going to improve her serve the day of a match enough for it to result in better service performance. Whatever players bring to the court in terms of their playing ability is what they will have to use that day. In the short-run, players have little real control over their ability.

PERFORMANCE FORMULA

Ability - Match Difficulty + Motivation = PERFORMANCE

Second, the difficulty of the match influences performance. Contributors to match difficulty include the ability of the opponent and external factors such as court conditions and weather such as temperature, wind, and sun. Players have no control over these factors.

Finally, motivation will impact performance. Motivation will directly affect players' long-term development and the level that players ultimately achieve. If players are highly motivated to improve their tennis, then they will put in the time and effort necessary to raise their game. Motivation will also influence the level of play when players walk onto the court for a match. If they're playing someone of nearly equal skill, it will not be ability that will determine the outcome of the match. Rather, it will be the player who works the hardest, who doesn't give up, and who plays their best when it counts. In other words, the player who is most motivated to win.

"There have never been any shortcuts for Courier; no quick fixes, no substitutes for back-breaking, muscle-straining, head-pounding hard work. There was no one else working harder than he was."

Tennis writer Richard Evans
speaking of Jim Courier

Signs of Low Motivation

Two questions players must ask themselves are, "How motivated am I?" and "Am I as motivated as I can be?" There are some common signs of low motivation. A lack of desire to practice as much as players could is one clear symptom of low motivation. This is especially important if their goals are high. Goals are great to have, but they will be unfulfilled if players are not motivated to achieve them. It's very important that motivation be consistent with goals. Are you willing to do what is necessary to reach your goals? If not, then you have two choices: increase your motivation so you can attain your goals or lower your goals to a level that, given your motivation, you will be able to reach.

Less than 100% effort in training is another warning sign of low motivation. When you go on court, do you give it your all? Do you work as hard as you can when you're practicing? Or do you not try that hard and put less than complete effort into your training? Skipping or shortening training sessions is also common for players with low motivation. If players are not motivated, it's easy to skip a practice because they just don't feel like it. If they do go to practice, they may only stay for a little while or they may goof around more than they hit balls. If you exhibit any of these symptoms of low motivation, you're not going to be the best player you can be. If you're not as motivated as you could be, you have to do two things. First, ask yourself why you're not working as hard as you could. Second, you must take active steps to increase your motivation in your tennis.

"With motivation, you can be involved or committed. Just like with ham and eggs: the chicken was involved, but the pig was committed. You have to be like the pig."

Martina Navratilova

Prime Motivation

Prime motivation means putting 100% of your time, effort, energy, and focus into all aspects of your tennis. It involves doing everything possible to become the best tennis player you can be. Prime motivation is based on what I call the three D's (see page 41). The first D stands for *direction*. Before you can attain prime motivation, you must first consider the different directions you can go in your tennis. You have three choices: stop playing completely, continue at your current level, or strive to be the best player you can be.

The second D represents *decision*. With these three choices of direction, you must select one direction in which to go. None of these directions are necessarily right or wrong, better or worse, they're simply your options. Your choice will dictate the amount of time and effort you will put into your tennis and how good a tennis player you will ultimately become.

The third D stands for *dedication*. Once you've made your decision, you must dedicate yourself to it. If your decision is to become the best player you can be, then this last step, dedication, will determine whether you have prime motivation. Your decision to be your best and your dedication to your tennis must be a top priority. Only by being completely dedicated to your direction and decision will you ensure that you have prime motivation.

THREE D'S

Direction → Decision → Dedication → MOTIVATION

Developing Motivation

Focus on your long-term goals. To be your best, you have to put a lot of time and effort into your game. But all of that time and effort is not always enjoyable. I call this the Grind, which involves having to hit a lot of tennis balls—forehands, backhands, volleys, serves—over and over and over again, well beyond the point that it is fun and exciting. If you let these immediate negative aspects of your tennis override the long-term benefits of working hard and putting in the time, your motivation is going to suffer and you're not going to get the most out of your tennis.

During those times when you're in the Grind and your motivation is suffering, focus on your long-term goals. Remind yourself why you're working so hard. Imagine exactly what you want to accomplish and tell yourself that the only way you'll be able to reach your goals is to go through the Grind. Also, try to generate the feelings of joy and fulfillment that you will experience when you reach your goals. This technique will distract you from the unpleasantness of the Grind, focus you on what you want to achieve, and generate some positive thoughts and emotions that will get you through the Grind.

Have a training partner. It's difficult to be highly motivated all of the time on your own. There are going to be some days when you don't feel like getting out there. Also, no matter how hard you push yourself, you will work that much harder if you have someone pushing you. That someone can be a coach, personal trainer, or parent. However, the best person to have is a regular training and hitting partner or your doubles partner. A training partner is someone at about your level of ability and with similar goals. You can work together to accomplish your goals. The chances are on any given day that one of you will be motivated. Even if you're not very psyched to practice on a particular day, you will still put in the time and effort because your partner is counting on you.

Focus on greatest competitor. Another way to keep yourself motivated is to focus on your greatest competitor. I have players identify who their biggest competition is and put his or her name or photo where they can see it every day. Ask yourself, "Am I working as hard as him/her?" Remember that only by working your hardest will you have a chance to overcome your greatest competitor.

Motivational cues. A big part of staying motivated involves generating positive emotions associated with your efforts and achieving your goals. A way to keep those feelings is with motivational cues such as inspirational phrases and photographs. If you come across some quote or picture that grabs you, place it where you can see it regularly such as in your bedroom, on your refrigerator door, or in your locker. Look at it periodically and allow yourself to experience the emotions it creates in you. These reminders and the emotions associated with them will inspire and motivate you to work hard in your tennis.

Set goals. There are few things more rewarding and motivating than setting a goal, putting effort toward the goal, and achieving the goal. The sense of accomplishment and validation of the effort makes you feel good and motivates you to strive higher. It's valuable to establish clear goals of what you want to accomplish in your tennis and how you will achieve those goals. Section V will describe how to do just that. Seeing that your hard work leads to progress and results should motivate you further to realize your tennis goals.

Daily questions. Finally, every day, you should ask yourself two questions. When you get up in the morning, ask, "What can I do today to become the best player I can be?" and before you go to sleep, ask, "Did I do everything possible today to become the best player I can be?" These two questions will remind you daily of what your goal is and will challenge you to be motivated to become your best.

The heart of motivation. A final point about motivation. The techniques I've just described are effective in increasing your motivation to play tennis. Motivation, though, is not something that can be given to you. Rather, motivation must ultimately come from within. You must simply want to play tennis. Motivation won't be a problem if you play tennis for the right reasons.

There are two things that should motivate you to play tennis. First, you should play because you have a great passion for the game. If you love the game, tennis will be important to you. Anything that you value, you will want to do to best of your ability.

Second, you should play because you love the process of the game. Not the winning, not the trophies, not the rankings, though they can certainly make you feel good. You should play because you just love to walk onto the court and hit tennis balls. There are not many professional players who don't love the Grind. It is that love that helps make them successful. If you truly love to play tennis, your motivation to work at all aspects of the game will be high.

"If you really want to achieve something in life, whatever you do to achieve the goal is never a sacrifice. It is simply something that you have to do."

Chris Evert

Twelve Laws of Prime Preparation

By achieving prime motivation, you take the first and most crucial step toward reaching your tennis goals. You can now follow what I call the Prime Motivation Progression (see below). Prime motivation pushes you to put in the necessary time and effort to be the best player you can be. This time and effort ensures that you have prime preparation, which I define as doing everything you can to be fully prepared to play your best.

PRIME MOTIVATION PROGRESSION

Prime Motivation → Prime Preparation → Prime Tennis

It is preparation that acts as the bridge between prime motivation and Prime Tennis. Without preparation, you will not have the tools or the experience to achieve your tennis goals. From my years of working with players at all levels of ability, I have developed twelve laws that must be understood and followed in order to accomplish prime preparation and achieve Prime Tennis.

First Law: *Matches are not won on the day you play, but rather in the days, weeks, and months before the matches.* Many players believe that if they're ready to go on the day of a match, then they're prepared to play their best and win. I have found that what happens on the day of the match has little impact on who wins or loses. Success will be determined by what players do in the days, weeks, and months leading up to the match. If you've put in the time and effort to developing your game physically, technically, tactically, and mentally, then, when you walk onto the court, you will have the skills and belief to play your best tennis. Even if things don't go well on the day of the match, for example, you get little sleep the night before or you're late to the courts, your prime preparation will override the immediate problems and bring your abilities to the fore.

Second Law: *Take responsibility for everything that can impact your tennis.* The only way that prime preparation can be achieved is if you know every area that influences your tennis. These areas include all of the components of physical (conditioning, rest, nutrition), technical (groundstrokes, serve, volley, footwork), tactical (baseline game, serve and volley), and mental (motivation, confidence, intensity, focus, and emotions) preparation. If you address every one of these areas, you can be sure that when you walk onto the court for a match, you will be totally prepared to play your best.

Third Law: *Preparation is the foundation of all physical, technical, tactical, and mental skills.* There is no magic to acquiring skills. There are no special techniques that enable you to learn faster or better. Developing skills of any sort requires three steps (see Positive Change Formula in Chapter Eight): (1) Awareness of what you're doing incorrectly and what is the proper execution; (2) Control to engage in the skills correctly; and (3) Repetition to ingrain the new skills. Only with this preparation will you be able to use those skills effectively and with confidence in a match.

Fourth Law: *The purpose of training is to develop effective skills and habits.* Training will ingrain in you a variety of physical, technical, tactical, and mental skills. If you want to experience Prime Tennis, you must be sure that you're developing skills and habits that will facilitate rather than interfere with Prime Tennis.

Fifth Law: *Practice makes perfect.* Whatever players practice, that is what they will become perfect at. If you practice effective skills and habits, you'll perfect skills and habits that will help you play your best. If you practice poor skills and habits, you'll become good at those and they will hurt your tennis. You will, in fact, become very good at being very bad; you will become highly skilled at ineffective skills. It's important that you're always practicing physical, technical, tactical, and mental skills that will allow you to achieve Prime Tennis.

Sixth Law: *Whatever players need to do in a match, they must first do it in practice.* Have you ever tried something new during a match because you thought it might help your game? Perhaps you decide to make a technical or tactical change in your game that you've never done before. It might not be a bad idea, but it probably didn't work. A match is simply not the place to try something different for the first time. If you haven't first learned it in training, you won't be able to use it in matches.

Another way to look at my sixth law is: whatever players do in training, that's what will come out in matches. The skills and habits you ingrain in practice are the ones that will come out in matches. You want to be sure that those skills and habits will help rather than hurt you. So you must figure out what you need to do in matches to play Prime Tennis and then learn and use them in training.

Seventh Law: *Prime preparation requires clear purpose, prime focus, and prime intensity.* It's impossible to engage in quality training unless three things are present. You must have a clear purpose that tells you what you're working on. If you don't know what you're doing, you will not be able to do it. Identifying the purpose of your preparation ensures that you put directed effort into that purpose. You must have prime focus which involves consistently maintaining focus on your purpose and avoiding distractions that will interfere with that focus. This means having cues to focus on that remind you of your purpose and ways of redirecting your focus when you become distracted. You must have prime intensity to achieve prime preparation. All of the mental techniques in the world won't work if your body is not prepared to execute the purpose you have identified. Having the awareness and control of your intensity will enable your body to ingrain the purpose and focus that you have worked on.

Eighth Law: *Players should train like they compete.* Whenever I give a seminar to players or coaches, I ask this question: Should you train like you compete or should you compete like you train? Most people say, you should compete like you train. Their response is understandable in some ways because if you could compete in the positive, relaxed, and focused way that you practice, then you would certainly play well. However, I would suggest that competing like you train is impossible for one simple reason: competition matters. Training is easy because you don't care that much if you make mistakes. If you play poorly in matches, though, you can feel really badly. This is because your ego is not on the line when you practice, but it is in matches. If you make mistakes in training, it is not that threatening to your view of yourself as a player. If you play poorly in matches, it hurts your "tennis self-esteem."

I believe that you should train like you compete. This means that you put as close to the same level of motivation, focus, and intensity into practice as is possible. It is probably unrealistic to think that you can train exactly like you compete. If you can get close to it, though, say 90%, then the last 10% that comes in a match is not a big leap. If you're training at 60-70%, then the jump to competitive motivation, focus, and intensity will be just too great and your game will suffer.

Ninth Law: *Consistent training leads to consistent competitive performance.* Consistency is an essential part of Prime Tennis and is one of the most important qualities that put the best players above the rest. The consistency in Prime Tennis comes from consistency in training. Referring back to my fourth law, consistency is one of those effective skills and habits that you need to develop in order to achieve Prime Tennis. Consistency relates to every aspects of tennis training and life. In addition to the obvious areas such as conditioning, technique, and tactics, it also pertains to areas including attitude, effort, focus, intensity, emotions, sleep, and diet. Any area that influences your tennis needs to be consistent before competitive tennis performance can be consistent.

Tenth Law: *The two most essential qualities necessary to achieve Prime Tennis are persistence and patience.* Skills take time to develop and you will experience plateaus, setbacks, and obstacles along the path toward improvement and Prime Tennis. You will get frustrated, impatient, and want to quit. If you let frustration and impatience overwhelm you and you give up, you will never achieve Prime Tennis. If you understand that progress takes time and that there is no way to hurry the learning process, you will have the patience to allow yourself to develop and experience Prime Tennis. Drawing on that patience, if you persist long enough in the face of the setbacks and obstacles, the improvement will come and you will achieve your goals of playing Prime Tennis.

Eleventh Law: *It takes 10 years and 10,000 hours to become an expert.* Dr. Anders Ericsson has studied expert performance in sports, music, chess, and other areas. He found two things that predicted the level that someone would achieve: how long they've been committed to the activity and how much they practiced. Applied to tennis, the longer you play and the more hours you practice, the better you will be. If you've ever seen the home movies of Andre Agassi hitting tennis balls when he was six years old, you understand why he is one of the best players in the world today.

Twelfth Law: *All preparation is devoted to readying players to play their best under the most demanding conditions in the most important match of their lives.* I'm not interested in you playing well in an unimportant match, under ideal conditions, against an opponent that you know you can defeat. The ultimate goal of Prime Tennis is for you play your best when it really matters, when the pressure is on, when your back is against the wall. Prime preparation will allow you to achieve Prime Tennis in your equivalent of a Davis Cup match in South America or a final at Centre Court Wimbledon.

"The ability to prepare to win is as important as the will to win."

University of Indiana basketball coach Bobby Knight

Chapter 4
Confidence

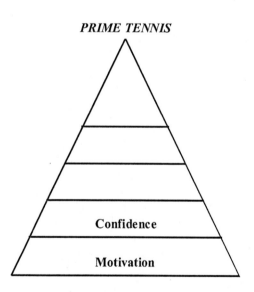

PRIME TENNIS

Confidence

Motivation

Confidence is the single most important mental factor for success in tennis. I define confidence as how strongly you believe you can play your best. Confidence impacts two levels of your game: your ability to hit specific shots and your ability to win. Confidence is so important because you may have all of the ability in the world to play well, but if you don't believe you have that ability, then you won't play up to that ability. For example, you may have the technical capabilities to hit a down-the-line backhand passing shot when an opponent comes to the net. Yet, you won't go for that shot if you don't have the confidence that you can make it.

Have you ever seen professionals who are ranked around 200 in the world play? If not, what you would see are outstanding players who generally have the ability to hit every shot. What then separates these players from those in the top ten if they have the same shots at their disposal? It is not their technical ability to hit a shot, for example, a drop shot or an offensive lob. Rather, it is their belief in their ability to hit that shot on the most important point in the most important match of their life. The best players have the confidence to hit the shot when they need it most. The lower ranked players don't have that belief, so they will try another shot that they have more confidence in even though it may not be the best shot for the situation in which they find themselves.

Too often players are their own worst enemy rather than their best ally on the court. Have you ever seen pros who, in pressure situations, seem to turn on themselves? They get frustrated and angry, and these negative reactions cause them to lose. Goran Ivanisevic and Venus Williams come to mind.

Whether you're your best ally or your worst enemy depends on your confidence. If you don't have much confidence in yourself, you probably don't think you can win a match. If that's the case and your opponent has confidence in their game, then you're in an impossible situation. As your worst enemy, you don't have a chance because it's two against zero on the court; you and your opponent against you. The only way you will have the chance to win is to become your best ally so that at least it is one against one. You have to allow yourself to be on your own side. Only then will you have any chance of winning the match.

"When confidence kicks in and you get to the tough parts of the match, you don't slow down. You just keep it coming."

Andre Agassi

Vicious Cycle or Upward Spiral

Not only does confidence impact performance directly, it also affects every other mental factor. To help illustrate this influence of confidence, think back to a time when you didn't have confidence in your tennis. You probably got caught in a vicious cycle of low confidence and play in which negative thinking led to poor play, which led to more negative thinking and even poorer play until your confidence was so low that you didn't even want to walk onto the court (see below).

This vicious cycle usually starts with a few missed shots or some losses. This poor play can lead to negative thinking and self-talk. "I'm terrible. I can't make that shot. I don't have a chance. I can't win today." You are becoming your own worst enemy.

You start to get nervous before a match because you believe you will lose. All of that anxiety hurts your confidence even more because you feel physically uncomfortable and there's no way you can play well when you're so uptight. The negative self-talk and anxiety causes negative emotions. You feel depressed, frustrated, angry, and helpless, all of which hurt your confidence more and cause you to play even worse.

The negative self-talk, anxiety, and emotions then hurt your focus. If you have low confidence, you can't help but focus on all of the negative things rather than on things that will enable you to play your best. All of this accumulated negativity hurts your motivation. As bad as you feel, you just want to get out of there. If you're thinking negatively, caught in a vicious cycle, feeling nervous, depressed, and frustrated, and can't focus, you're not going to have much fun playing tennis and you're not going to play well.

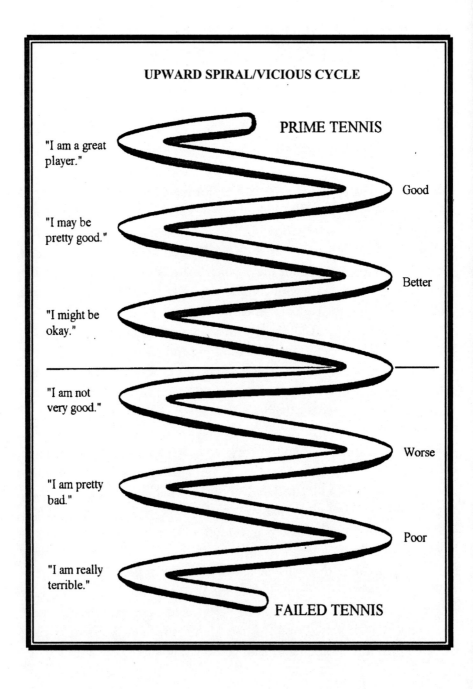

In contrast to those times when you have had low confidence, recall when you have been really confident in your game. Your self-talk is positive. "I'm a good player. I can hit that shot. I can win." Instead of being your worst enemy, you're your best ally on the court.

With the positive self-talk, rather than being dragged down into the vicious cycle, you begin an upward spiral of high confidence and performance in which positive thinking leads to better performance, which leads to more positive thinking and even better performance (see page 52).

All of the positive talk gets you feeling relaxed and energized as you walk onto the court. You have a lot of positive emotions such as happiness, joy and excitement. You focus on things you need to play your best. Competing is actually an enjoyable experience for you.

All of the positive thoughts and feelings motivate you to play. If you're thinking positively, riding an upward spiral, feeling relaxed and energized, experiencing happiness and excitement, and are focused on playing your best, you're going to have a lot of fun playing tennis and you're going to play well.

Why Players Lose Confidence

Remember that confidence is the belief players have in their ability to play well. Anything that counters that belief will hurt their confidence. The most disruptive thing to hurt confidence is failure of any kind. Failure can mean making a number of errors early in a match, for example, missing four forehands in the first two games. This will cause players to lose confidence in their forehand and may cause them to become tentative or to avoid hitting forehands the rest of the match. Failure can also mean having lost early in recent tournaments. Players who have played poorly may question their ability and may become unwilling to take risks and hit out on the ball.

Unrealistic expectations can also hurt confidence. You should make sure that your confidence is realistic. In other words, is your confidence in your ability consistent with your actual ability? If it is not, then you'll have unrealistic expectations that can never be reached. You may be overly critical of your play based on those unreasonable beliefs about your ability, believing that you didn't play as well as you should have instead of simply having played up to your realistic ability.

Lack of experience or skills can also hurt confidence. If you have not played very much or have not competed at the current level in which you're playing, you may not have the experience to adequately evaluate how well you should play. Often, play that is interpreted as poor is actually just the opponent playing at a higher level. This is particularly likely if you're playing at a new level above where you had previously competed. You may simply lack the necessary experience to be competitive at that level. Without this realization, instead of adjusting your perceptions accordingly, you'll assume that you're playing poorly and your confidence will decline.

> *"There are things we are physically capable of doing but push away from because our minds tell us to. That's the mind's negative programming."*
>
> Former All-Pro football
> player Jim Page

Confidence is a Skill

A misconception that many players have is that confidence is something that is inborn or that if they don't have it at an early age, they will never have confidence. In reality, confidence is a skill, much like technical skills, that can be learned. Just like with any type of skill, confidence is developed through practice and experience.

The problem many players have with confidence is that they violate my fourth and fifth laws of preparation. They developed ineffective confidence skills and habits, and by practicing being negative, they became perfect at being negative. They became highly skilled at something that actually hurts their tennis.

If a player has a bad technical habit, for example, he brings his racquet back too high on his forehand to hit topspin, he probably has hit his forehand that way for a long time. He has become skilled at hitting his forehand the wrong way. The same holds true for confidence. Players can become skilled at being negative.

To change bad confidence skills, players must retrain the way they think. They have to practice good confidence skills regularly until the old negative habits have been broken and they have learned and ingrained the new positive skills of confidence. The techniques described below will help you in this process by giving you specific strategies can use to unlearn bad habits and learn good skills.

A question I'm often asked is, "Do you become confident by succeeding or do you succeed from being confident?" I believe that success in tennis comes from confidence. You don't just go from 0% confidence to 100% confidence in one big step. Rather, it's a building process in which confidence leads to success which reinforces the confidence which, in turn, leads to more success. For example, a player may only have 40% confidence in her backhand. By working on her backhand and using the confidence building techniques described on the following pages, her confidence goes up to 60%. Yet, all of the positive thinking in the world won't help if she doesn't have experiences to confirm her beliefs. With her confidence now at 60%, she's able to have greater focus and intensity in her training, which results in further improvement in her backhand. Her hard work and progress raises her confidence to 80%. Her improved preparation and greater confidence results in a more consistent and effective backhand in matches. Her improved backhand and her success in matches then increases her confidence to near 100%. Her confidence in her overall game also rises because her backhand improves her game as a whole.

Prime Confidence

Prime confidence is a deep, lasting, and resilient belief in one's ability. With prime confidence, players are able to stay confident even when they're not playing well. Prime confidence keeps them positive, motivated, intense, focused, and emotionally in control when they need to be. Players are not negative and uncertain in difficult matches and they're not over-confident in easy matches. It also encourages players to seek out pressure situations and to view difficult conditions and tough opponents as challenges to pursue. Prime confidence enables players to play at their highest level consistently.

Prime confidence is a belief, not a certainty, that players can win. It is the confidence that if players do the right things, they will prevail. Prime confidence demonstrates faith and trust in their ability and their preparation. It does not, however, lead players to know, expect, or have to win. This belief can produce arrogance and overconfidence. It can also cause players to become too focused on winning the match instead of playing the match. This perception can lead to self-imposed pressure and a fear of losing.

"I'm confident on the court. I think it's the mark of
a great player to be confident in tough situations."

John McEnroe

Progression of Confidence

I have identified a four-step progression that will lead you along the upward spiral of confidence. Each step alone can enhance your confidence, but if you use all of them together, you'll find your confidence growing stronger and more quickly. The ultimate goal of prime confidence is to develop a strong and resilient belief in your tennis ability so that you have the confidence to go for your shots and believe you can win in the most important point of the most important match of your life.

Preparation breeds confidence. Preparation is the foundation of confidence. If you walk onto the court believing that you have done everything you can to play your best, you will have confidence in your ability to play well. This preparation includes the physical, technical, tactical, and mental parts of the game. If you have developed these areas as fully as you can, you will have faith that you will be able to use those skills gained from preparation to play as well as you can. The more of these areas you cover in your preparation, the more confidence you will breed in yourself.

Mental skills reinforce confidence. As I have indicated previously, confidence is a skill that develops with practice. A meaningful way to strengthen the confidence you've built through preparation is to use mental skills that provide repetition of the confidence. These mental skills include goal setting to bolster motivation, positive self-talk and body language to fortify the confident beliefs, intensity control to combat confidence-depleting anxiety, keywords to maintain focus and avoid distractions, and emotional control to stay calm under pressure. These mental skills are described throughout Section III.

Adversity ingrains confidence. It's one thing to be confident when you're playing well and things are going your way. It is an entirely different challenge to maintain your belief in yourself when you're faced with adversity. To more deeply ingrain confidence in your tennis, you should expose yourself to as much adversity as possible. Adversity can involve anything that makes you uncomfortable and takes you out of your comfort zone. Adversity can be environmental obstacles such as bad weather including wind and sun, poor court conditions, or a playing surface on which you don't usually play well. Adversity can also involve your opponent, for example, someone who is a little better than you are, or an opponent who has a style of play that frustrates you, or someone who you believe you should defeat but who always seems to get the better of you.

Playing under adversity has several essential benefits. It demonstrates your competence to play well under difficult conditions. Adversity teaches you additional skills you can use to perform at a higher level. It also prepares you for adversity that you will inevitably experience when you play matches. All of these aspects of adversity will ingrain confidence in your tennis.

Success validates confidence. All of the previous steps in building confidence would go for naught if you did not then play well and win. Success validates the confidence you have developed in your ability. It demonstrates that your belief in your ability is well-founded. Success further strengthens your confidence, making it more resilient in the face of adversity and poor play. Finally, success rewards your efforts to build confidence, encouraging you to continue to work hard and develop your game.

> *"The center of my confidence and my tennis game is 100 percent in my physical fitness. I get a lot more focused when I'm in shape."*
>
> Andre Agassi

Building Confidence

You now see the importance of having prime confidence. Let's discuss how you can develop your confidence with Prime Tennis techniques. One mistake that players often make is they wait to do mental training until after they've lost confidence. You don't wait to get hurt before you start doing physical training. You don't wait to develop a technical problem before you work on technique. You do them beforehand to prevent the problems. The same thing holds true for building confidence.

Walk the walk. One thing I've noticed about working with pros is that they carry themselves a certain way. They move and walk with confidence. A first step in developing confidence is to learn to "walk the walk." How you carry yourself, move, and walk affects what you think and how you feel. If your body is down, your thoughts and feelings will be negative. If your body is up, your thoughts and feelings will be positive. It's hard to feel down when your body is up. Walking the walk involves moving with your head high, chin up, eyes forward, shoulders back, arms swinging, and a bounce in your step. You look and move like a winner.

In contrast, not walking the walk involves your head, eyes, and shoulders down, feet dragging, and no energy in your step. You look and move like a loser. To give you a feeling of what this is like, try walking the walk and saying negative things about yourself. As you will see, it's difficult to do because your thoughts are inconsistent with what your body is signaling to you. Then try not walking the walk and saying positive things. Again, it's difficult because your thoughts conflict with what your body is doing.

Related to walking the walk, you can influence your thoughts and feelings with your body language. To get more positive, clench your fist, pump your arms, slap your thigh. This positive body language will affect your thinking and emotions, especially if you combine it with high-energy positive self-talk.

By the way, when you walk the walk, not only are you telling yourself that you're confident, but you're also communicating confidence to your opponent. There's nothing more discouraging than to be ahead, but to look across the net at someone who is positive, fired up, and motivated to keep fighting. There is also nothing more invigorating than to see your opponent looking like they've already lost. By not walking the walk, you're not only hurting your confidence, but you're also building your opponent's confidence.

Talk the talk. In addition to walking the walk, you can also learn to "talk the talk." What you say to yourself affects what you think and how you feel. If your talk is negative, your thoughts and feelings will be negative. If your talk is positive, your thoughts and feelings will be positive. It's hard to think and feel negative when you're talking positively. Don't say,

"I don't have a chance today." Say, "I'm going to play hard today. I'm going to play the best I can." That will get you positive and fired up. By talking the talk, you're also being your own best ally. You're showing yourself that your opponent may be against you, but you're on your side. If you're saying positive things out loud during a match, you're also letting your opponent know that if you're going to lose, they will have to defeat you, you will not defeat yourself.

Conversely, not talking the talk includes "I'm going to play terribly today," "I may do okay," and "I don't know how I'll play today." If you say these things to yourself, you're convincing yourself that you have no chance. With that attitude, you really have no chance because not only is your opponent planning on defeating you, but you're planning on losing to them as well. Even worse, if you talk negatively out loud during a match, you're basically saying to your opponent that you've already lost.

Balance the scales. When I work with players, I always chart the number of positive and negative things they say or do during a match. In most cases, the negatives far outnumber the positives. In an ideal world, I would love to eliminate all negatives and have players only express positives. But this is the real world and any player who cares about the game is going to feel and express anger, frustration, and helplessness occasionally.

In dealing with this reality, you should learn to *balance the scales.* If you're going to be negative when you miss shots and lose points, you should also be positive when you hit good shots and win points. The immediate goal is to increase the positives. This means rewarding yourself when you play well. If you beat yourself up over an error, why shouldn't you pat yourself on the back when you hit a winner. Pump your fist, slap your leg, say, "yes," when you hit a good shot. It will psych you up and make you feel positive and excited.

Once you've balanced the scales by increasing your positives, your next goal is to tip the scales in the positive direction by reducing the negatives. Ask why you're so hard on yourself when you miss a shot. The best players in the world make dozens of errors in matches that they win. Why shouldn't it be okay for you to miss shots too?

Become aware of your negative self-talk and body language. Do things that counter the negativity. For example, after you miss a shot, instead of dropping your head, shrugging your shoulders and saying, "I stink," try bouncing up and down, pumping your fist, and saying, "Come on!"

This step of tipping the scales toward positives is so important because of some recent research that found that negative experiences such as negative self-talk, negative body language, and negative emotions carry more weight than positive experiences. In fact, it takes 12 positive experiences to equal one negative experience. What this means is that for every negative expression you make on the court, whether saying something negative or throwing your racquet or screaming in frustration, you must express yourself positively 12 times to counteract that one negative expression.

Remember, your self-talk, how you walk, and your body language are skills. If your scale is tipped heavily to the negative side, you have become very skilled at these negative expressions. Like changing any skill, to get rid of these bad ones, you have to identify better skills, make a commitment to changing them, and practice the positive skills until they're ingrained and automatic.

Thought-stopping. As a well-known psychologist once said, "We become what we think of most of the time." If you're always thinking negatively, then you will likely fail. Another useful technique to reduce your negative thinking and develop your positive thinking is called thought-stopping. This strategy involves replacing your negative self-talk with positive self-talk. Using the Thought Stopping Exercise (see page 63), list the negative statements you commonly say to yourself when you're practicing and competing. Next, indicate where and in what situations you say the negative things. This will help you become aware of the situations in which you're most likely to be negative. Then, list positive statements with which you can replace them. For example, after a bad day, you might say "I had a horrible match." Instead, replace that negative statement with something more positive such as "I'll work hard and do better in the next match."

The thought-stopping sequence goes as follows. When you start to think or say something negative; say "stop" or "positive," then replace it with a positive statement. As you learn this new skill, you'll become aware of yourself saying negative things before you actually say them and you'll automatically say something positive.

THOUGHT-STOPPING EXERCISE

Directions: In the space below, list common negative thoughts that you have, where and when they occur, and positive statements to place them.

Negative Thoughts	Time, Place Situation	Positive Replacement
1.		
2.		
3.		
4.		
5.		
6.		
7.		
8.		

Tennis Player's Litany. The Tennis Player's Litany is a group of self-statements used to teach positive thinking and increase confidence (see page 65). The litany is like a hitting drill in which you're focusing on ingraining good technical skills. The litany provides the necessary repetition to instill positive thinking skills.

As I've indicated before, players are often their own worst enemy. They have a considerable amount of negative thinking and negative self-talk, and this negativity becomes a bad habit. The more players say negative things, the better they become at being negative. The litany retrains the bad habit of negativity into a good skill of positive thinking. As with any kind of habit, the only way to correct negative thinking is to practice being positive over and over and over again.

A comment I often get from players when they start using the litany is that they don't believe what they're saying. This is just like the hitting drill in which they're making a technical correction. In a sense, their muscles don't "believe" the new skill either. In time, though, the new skill is learned and their muscles come to "believe" it. The same holds true for the positive self-statements. By repeating the litany enough times, players start believing it. Just like that improved forehand, when they get into a match situation, the new skill of positive thinking will emerge and it will improve their game.

The important thing about the Tennis Player's Litany is not only to say it, but to say it like you mean it. For example, I could say "I love to compete, I'm a great player," but I may not sound very convincing. If I say it like I mean it, then I'm more likely to start believing what I'm saying. Saying the litany with conviction also generates positive emotions and physical feelings that will reinforce its positive message.

A great thing about the Tennis Player's Litany is that you can personalize it to your needs. Create your own litany of positive self-statements that means something to you. Then, say the litany out loud every morning and every night. Also, say the litany before you train and compete.

TENNIS PLAYER'S LITANY

Directions: Repeat the litany when you wake up in the morning, before practice and matches, before you go to sleep at night, or whenever you have doubts or lose confidence in your tennis. Remember to say the litany out loud like you mean it. Also, personalize the litany by adding positive statements that are important to you.

I LOVE TO PLAY TENNIS.

I AM COMMITTED TO BECOMING THE BEST PLAYER I CAN BE.

I THINK AND TALK POSITIVELY.

I GIVE 100% FOCUS AND INTENSITY WHEN I PRACTICE AND PLAY.

I AM MY BEST ALLY WHEN I PLAY.

IF I FOCUS ON PLAYING MY BEST RATHER THAN ON WINNING OR LOSING, I WILL SUCCEED.

I STRIVE TO PLAY MY BEST WHEN THE PRESSURE IS ON.

I PLAY HARD WHETHER I AM AHEAD OR BEHIND IN A MATCH.

IF I GIVE MY BEST EFFORT, I AM A WINNER.

Keywords. Another useful way to develop your confidence is to use key-words which remind you to be positive and confident. Make a list of words that make you feel positive and good. Then, write them on your equipment where they're visible during practice and matches. Also, put keywords in noticeable places where you live such as in your bedroom, on your refrigerator door, or in your locker. When you look at a keyword, say it to yourself. Just like the Tennis Player's Litany, every time you see it, it will sink in further until you truly believe it.

Using negative thinking positively. Even though I very much emphasize being positive at all times, the fact is, you can't always be positive. You don't always play as well as you want and there is going to be some nega-tive thinking. This awareness was brought home to me at a USTA national camp I worked at not long ago. During the camp, I was constantly emphasizing being positive and not being negative. One night at dinner, several of the players came up to and said that sometimes things do just stink and you can't be positive. I realized that negative thinking is normal when you don't play well and some negative thinking is healthy. It means you care about playing poorly and want to play better. Negative thinking can be motivating as well because it's no fun to play poorly and lose. I got to thinking about how players could use negative thinking in a positive way. I came up with an important distinction that will determine whether negative thinking helps or hurts your tennis.

There are two types of negative thinking: give-up negative thinking and fire-up negative thinking. Give-up negative thinking involves feelings of loss and despair and helplessness, for example, "It's over. I can't win this match." You dwell on past mistakes and failures. It lowers your motivation and con-fidence, and it takes your focus away from playing your best. Your intensity also drops because basically you're surrendering and accepting defeat. There is never a place on the tennis court for give-up negative thinking.

In contrast, fire-up negative thinking involves feelings of anger and energy, of being psyched up, for example, "I am playing so badly. I hate playing this way" (said with anger and intensity). You look to doing better in the future because you hate playing poorly and losing. Fire-up negative thinking increases your motivation to fight and turn the match around. Your intensity goes up and you're bursting with energy. Your focus is on attacking and defeating your opponent.

Fire-up negative thinking can be a positive way to turn your game around. if you're going to be negative, make sure you use fire-up negative thinking. Don't use it too much though. Negative thinking and negative emotions require a lot of energy and that energy should be put in a more positive direction for your training and matches. Also, it doesn't feel very good to be angry all of the time.

> *"You tell your mind what to do and if you're able to fuel your mind with positive thoughts and confidence, you'll achieve amazing things."*
>
> 1984 Olympic marathon champion Joan Benoit-Samuelson

Confidence Challenge

The real test of confidence is how you respond when things are not going your way. I call this the Confidence Challenge. It's easy to stay confident when you're playing well, when the conditions are ideal, and when you're playing someone whom you're better than. But as I said earlier, an inevitable part of tennis is that you'll have some down periods. What separates the best from the rest is that the best players are able to maintain their confidence when they're not at the top of their games. By staying confident, they continue to play their game rather than try to change it because they know that, in time, their game will come around.

Most players when they play poorly lose their confidence and get caught in the vicious cycle of low confidence and performance. Once they slip into that downward spiral, they rarely can get out of it. In contrast, players with prime confidence maintain their confidence and seek out ways to return to their previous level. All players will go through periods where they don't play well. The skill is not getting caught in the vicious cycle and being able to get out of the down periods quickly.

The Confidence Challenge can be thought of as a Prime Tennis skill that can be developed. Learning to respond positively to the Confidence Challenge comes from exposing yourself to demanding situations, difficult conditions, and tough opponents in training and matches and practicing positive responses.

There are several key aspects of mastering the Confidence Challenge. First, you need to develop the attitude that demanding situations are challenges to be sought out rather than threats to be avoided. When you're faced with a Confidence Challenge you must see it as an opportunity to become a better player. You also need to believe that experiencing challenges is a necessary part of becoming the best player you can be. You have to realize that, at first, these challenges are going to be uncomfortable because they're difficult and unfamiliar. As you expose yourself to more challenges, they will become less threatening and more comfortable.

With this perspective, you should seek out every possible challenge in training and matches. Be sure you're well-prepared to meet the challenges. You can't master the Confidence Challenge if you don't have the preparation and skills to do so. Stay positive and motivated in the face of the difficulties. Don't allow yourself to be sucked into the vicious cycle. Then, focus on what you need to do to overcome the challenge rather than on how difficult it may be or how you may fail. Also, accept that you'll make mistakes and may not fully succeed when faced with a challenge for the first time. Don't take this as a failure, but rather as an experience you can learn from to improve next time. Finally, and most importantly, never, ever give up!

"Confidence is the difference in a decisive set."

Chris Evert

Chapter 5
Intensity

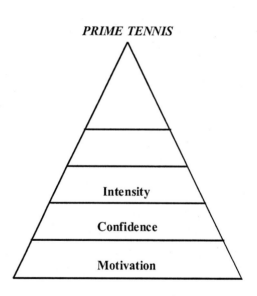

PRIME TENNIS

Intensity

Confidence

Motivation

Intensity may be the most important contributor to performance once your match begins. It's so important because all of the motivation, confidence, focus, and emotions in the world won't help you if your body is not physiologically capable of doing what it needs to do in order for you to play your best.

Simply put, intensity is the amount of physiological activity you experience in your body including heart rate, respiration, and adrenaline. Intensity is a continuum that ranges from sleep (very relaxed) to terror (very anxious). Somewhere in between those two extremes is the level of intensity at which you play your best tennis.

Intensity is made up of two components. First, there is the physical experience of intensity, that is, what you actually feel in your body when you're playing a match. Are you calm or filled with energy? Are you relaxed or tense? Second, there is your perception of the intensity. In other words, do you perceive the intensity positively or negatively? Two players can feel the exact same thing physiologically, but interpret those physical feelings in very different ways. One may view the intensity as excitement and it will help his performance. Another may see the intensity as anxiety and it will hurt his performance.

The physical experience and the perception of intensity are affected by several mental factors. If you are not confident, feeling frustrated and angry, and focusing on winning rather than on playing your best, you will see the intensity as negative. In contrast, if you are confident and positive, happy and excited, and focused on playing well, the intensity will be perceived as positive.

"It's all about intensity. If you lose it, even just for a little while, you're in trouble."

Former NBA player
Doc Rivers

Signs of Over- and Under-intensity

Intensity produces a wide variety of physical and mental symptoms that can help you recognize when your intensity is too high or too low. By being aware of these signs, you will be able to know when you're not playing at prime intensity and can take steps to reach that ideal level.

Overintensity. Muscle tension and breathing difficulties are the most common signs of overintensity. Most players indicate that when they're too intense, they feel tension in their shoulders and their legs, which happen to be the two most important physical areas in tennis. If their shoulders are tense, the motion of their groundstrokes and serve will shorten and players won't be able to hit with ease, accuracy, or power. When their legs get tense, players lose the ability to move with quickness and agility.

Many players also report that their breathing becomes short and choppy when they get nervous. This restriction in breathing means that they're not getting enough oxygen into their system so they will tire quickly. I've also found that the smoothness of players' strokes tend to mirror their breathing. If their breathing is long and smooth, so will their strokes be. If their breathing is abrupt and choppy, their strokes will be jerky and uncomfortable.

Players who are overly intense often exhibit poor posture and a stiff gait. Muscle tension causes their shoulders to rise (try hitting a serve with your shoulders by your ears) or their body to seem to close up. Players make more errors when they're overly intense because anxiety disrupts coordination. Overintensity interferes with motor control that affects strokes and movement. Players who are anxious also increase the pace of the match. They take little time between points and all of their movements tend to be rushed and frantic. If opponents are taking their time between points, overly intense players become impatient at the slow pace.

Overintensity negatively influences players mentally as well. Anxiety lowers confidence and causes doubts in ability. The physical and mental discomfort produces negative emotions such as frustration, anger, and depression. The anxiety, doubts, and negative emotions hurt focus by drawing players' attention away from playing their best and onto how badly they feel.

Underintensity. Though not as common, players can also experience underintensity during a match. The most common symptom of underintensity is low energy and lethargy. Players lack the adrenaline they need to give their best effort. Though not as discomforting as overintensity, underintensity hurts performance equally because players lack the physical requisites such as strength, stamina, and agility to meet the demands of tennis.

Mentally, underintensity undermines motivation. Players just don't feel like being out on the court. The lack of interest caused by too low intensity also impairs their focus because they're easily distracted and have difficulty staying focused on their game.

> *"I can't press, I can't get too tight, because then there's a danger that I'll try so hard to do well that I'll mess up."*
>
> former NFL great
> Marcus Allen

Line Between Intensity and Tensity

The ultimate goal of prime intensity is to find the precise line between intensity and tensity. The closer players can get to that line, the more their bodies will work for them in achieving Prime Tennis. If players cross the line to tensity, their bodies will no longer be physically capable of playing Prime Tennis. Great players have the ability to do two things related to this line. First, they have a better understanding of where that line is, so they can "tightrope walk" on it, thereby maximizing what their bodies can give them. Second, they're able to stay on that line longer than other players, which enables them to play at a consistently higher level for longer periods of time.

"I love to hit when the pressure's on. I enjoy the excitement. I try harder. I concentrate more."

Former baseball great
Reggie Jackson

Prime Intensity

Prime intensity is the ideal amount of physiological activity necessary for you to play your best tennis. It is also the level of intensity that you perceive as most positive and beneficial to your tennis. Unfortunately, there is no one ideal level of intensity for every player. Prime intensity is individual; it's different for everyone. Some players play best relaxed. Others play best energized, but not too psyched up. Still others play best unbelievably intense and fired up. You must find out the level of intensity that enables you to play your best tennis.

You have several goals in developing prime intensity. First, to learn what is your prime intensity. Then, to recognize the signs of overintensity and underintensity. Next, to identify match situations in which your intensity may go up or down. Finally, to take active steps to reach and maintain prime intensity throughout your matches.

Your intensity is much like the thermostat maintaining the most comfortable temperature in your house. You always notice when your house is too warm or too cold because you're sensitive to changes in temperature. When the temperature becomes uncomfortable, you adjust the thermostat to a more comfortable level. You can think of your intensity as your internal temperature that needs to be adjusted periodically. You need to be sensitive to when your intensity is no longer comfortable, in other words, it's not allowing you to play your best. You can then use the intensity control techniques I'll be describing to you to raise or lower your intensity to your prime level.

"Intensity has always been the strongest part of my game."

Jim Courier

Determining Prime Intensity

Using the Intensity Identification form (see page 76), you can identify what is your prime intensity. First, think back to several matches in which you played very well. Recall your level of intensity. Were you relaxed, energized, or really fired up? Then remember the thoughts, emotions, and physical feelings you experienced during these matches. Were you positive or negative, happy or angry, relaxed or tense? Second, think back to several matches in which you played poorly. Recall your level of intensity. Remember the thoughts, emotions, and physical feelings you had in these matches. If you're like most players, a distinct pattern will emerge. When you play well, you have a particular level of intensity. This is your prime intensity. There are also common thoughts, emotions, and physical feelings associated with playing well. In contrast, when you're playing poorly, there is a very different level of intensity, either higher or lower than your prime intensity. There are also decidedly different thoughts, emotions, and physical feelings.

Another useful way to help you understand your prime intensity is to experiment with different levels of intensity in practice and see how the differing intensity impacts your tennis. Here is a good exercise you can use to learn more about your prime intensity:

Let's say you're working on your groundstrokes. Break up the drill into three segments involving approximately 25 balls each. The first segment will emphasize low intensity. Before you begin the drill, take several slow, deep breaths, relax your muscles, and focus on calming thoughts (e.g., "Easy does it," "Cool and calm."). Don't bounce on your feet before you begin the drill. As you start the drill, stay focused on keeping your body relaxed and calm.

The second segment will focus on moderate intensity. Before the drill, take a few deep, but stronger breaths, walk around a bit, and focus on more energetic thoughts (e.g., "Let's go," "Pick it up."). Before the drill, bounce on your feet lightly and feel your intensity picking up. During the drill, pay attention to feeling the intensity and energy in your body and keeping your body moving between hits.

The final segment will highlight high intensity. Before the drill, take several deep, forced breaths with special emphasis on a hard and aggressive exhale, start bouncing up and down immediately, and repeat intense thoughts (e.g., "Fire it up," "Get after it."), saying these out loud with energy and force. Feel the high level of intensity and energy as you begin the drill, and focus on maintaining the intensity with constant foot movement and high-energy self-talk.

I encourage you to use this exercise for several days so you can see clearly how your intensity impacts your game. As with the Intensity Identification form, you will probably see a pattern emerge in which you move and hit the ball better at one of the three levels of intensity. With this knowledge, you will have a good sense of your prime intensity and can then use that information to recognize when you're not at prime intensity and when you need to adjust your intensity to a prime level.

INTENSITY IDENTIFICATION

Directions: In the space below, indicate the mental and physical factors that are related to your best (prime intensity) and worst (overintensity or underintensity) matches. At the bottom, summarize the positive and negative factors that distinguish your prime from poor intensity.

	Best Matches	**Worst Matches**
Importance of match		
Difficulty of opponent		
Match conditions		
Thoughts		
Emotions		
Physical feelings		

Psych-Down Techniques

When you're in a pressure situation during a match, it's natural for your intensity to go up and for you to feel nervous. If you want to play your best, you have to take active steps to get your intensity back to its prime level. There are several simple techniques you can use to help you get your intensity back under control.

Deep breathing. When players experience overintensity, one of the first things that's disrupted is their breathing. It becomes short and choppy and they don't get the oxygen their body needs to perform its best. The most basic way to lower their intensity then is to take control of their breathing again by focusing on taking slow, deep breaths.

Deep breathing has several important benefits. It ensures that you get enough oxygen so your body can function well. By getting more oxygen into your body, you will relax, feel better, and it will give you a greater sense of control. This increased comfort will give you more confidence and enable you to more easily combat negative thoughts. It will also help you let go of negative emotions such as frustration and allow you to regain positive emotions such as excitement. Focusing on your breathing also acts to take your mind off of things that may be interfering with your tennis and back onto things that will enable you to play better.

Deep breathing should be a part of your between-point and changeover routines (to be discussed further in Chapter Nine). One place in particular where deep breathing can be especially valuable to reduce intensity is before you serve. If you take two deep breaths before each service point, you ensure that your body is relaxed and comfortable, and you're focused on something that will help your serve.

Muscle relaxation. The most common sign of overintensity is muscle tension. This is the most crippling physical symptom because if your muscles are tight and stiff, you won't be able to hit the ball with either power or accuracy, or move with speed or agility. There are two muscle relaxation techniques, passive relaxation and active relaxation, you can use off-court or, in a shortened form, on changeovers or between points. Similar to deep breathing, muscle relaxation is beneficial because it allows you to regain control of your body and to make you feel more comfortable physically. It also offers the same mental and emotional advantages as does deep breathing.

Passive relaxation involves imagining that tension is a liquid that fills your muscles creating discomfort that interferes with your body performing its best. By imagining that you have drain plugs on the bottom of your feet, the tension can drain out of your body and you can attain a desired state of relaxation.

To prepare for passive relaxation, lie down in a comfortable position in a quiet place where you won't be disturbed. Use the passive relaxation procedure described on page 80. You can memorize the procedure, have someone guide you through it, or record it on an audiotape and listen to it on your own. As you go through the passive relaxation procedure, take your time, focus on your breathing and your muscles, feel the tension leave your body, and, at the end, focus on your overall state of mental calmness and physical relaxation.

Active relaxation is used when your body is very tense and you can't relax your muscles with passive relaxation. When your intensity is too high and your muscles are tight, it's difficult to just relax them. So instead of trying to relax your muscles, do just the opposite. Tighten them more, then release them. Our muscles work on what is called an opponent principle process. For example, before a match, your muscle tension might be at an 8, where 1 is totally relaxed and 10 is very tense, but you play best at a 4. By further tightening your muscles up to a 10 , the natural reaction is for your muscles to rebound back past 8 toward a more relaxed 4. So, making your muscles more tense actually causes them to become more relaxed.

Active relaxation typically involves tightening and relaxing four major muscle groups: face and neck, arms and shoulders, chest and back, and buttocks and legs. It can also be individualized to focus on particular muscles that trouble you the most.

To get ready for active relaxation follow the same preparations as I described for passive relaxation, Use the active relaxation procedure described on page 81. The most important part of active relaxation is learning to tell the difference between states of tension and relaxation. As you go through the active relaxation procedure, focus on the differences between tension and relaxation, be aware of how you were able to induce a greater feeling of relaxation, and, at the end, focus on your overall state of mental calmness and physical relaxation.

These two relaxation procedures can also be used on-court in an abbreviated form. Between points, you can stop for five seconds and allow the tension to drain out of tense parts of your body. Just before you serve, you can do a set of active relaxation on your shoulders. During changeovers, you can put a towel over your head and use either technique to reduce the tension you may be feeling.

PASSIVE RELAXATION

Imagine there are drain plugs on the bottom of your feet. When you open them, all the tension will drain out of your body and you will become very, very relaxed. Take a slow, deep breath.

Now, undo those plugs. Feel the tension begin to drain out of your body. Down from the top of your head, past your forehead, your face and neck; you're becoming more and more relaxed. The tension drains out of your jaw and down past your neck. Now your face and your neck are warm and relaxed and comfortable. Take a slow, deep breath.

The tension continues to drain out of your upper body, past your hands and forearms, and out of your upper arms and shoulders. Now your hands, arms and shoulders are warm and relaxed and comfortable. Take a slow, deep breath.

The tension continues to drain out of your upper body, past your chest and upper back, down past your stomach and lower back, and your upper body is becoming more and more relaxed. There is no more tension left in your upper body. Now your entire upper body is warm and relaxed and comfortable. Take a slow, deep breath.

The tension continues to drain out of your lower body, past your buttocks and down past your thighs, and your knees. Your lower body is becoming more and more relaxed. The tension drains out of your calves. There is almost no more tension left in your body and the last bit of tension drains past your ankles, the balls of your feet, and your toes. Now do a brief survey of your body from head to toe to ensure that there is no more tension left in your body. Your entire body is warm and relaxed and comfortable. Now replace the plugs so that no tension can get back in. Take a slow, deep breath. Feel the calm and relaxation envelop you. Enjoy that feeling and remember what it feels like to be completely relaxed.

ACTIVE RELAXATION

When I say tight, I want you to tighten that body part for five seconds; when I say loose, I want you to relax it.

First, your buttocks and legs. Tight...loose. Feel the relaxation. Take a slow, deep breath. Once again with the buttocks and legs. Tight...loose. The muscles in your buttocks and legs are warm and relaxed. Feel the difference between the states of tension and relaxation in your buttocks and legs. Take a slow, deep breath.

Now your chest and back. Tight...loose. Feel the relaxation. Take a slow, deep breath. Once again with the chest and back. Tight...loose. The muscles in your chest and back are warm and relaxed. Feel the difference between the states of tension and relaxation in your chest and back. Take a slow, deep breath.

Now your arms and shoulders. Tight...loose. Feel the relaxation. Take a slow, deep breath. Once again with the arms and shoulders. Tight...loose. The muscles in your arms and shoulders are warm and relaxed. Feel the difference between the states of tension and relaxation in your arms and shoulders. Take a slow, deep breath.

Now your face and neck. Tight...loose. Feel the relaxation. Take a slow, deep breath. Once again with the face and neck. Tight...loose. The muscles in your face and neck are warm and relaxed. Feel the difference between the states of tension and relaxation in your face and neck. Take a slow, deep breath.

Now every muscle in your body. Be sure that every muscle is as tight as you can get it. Tight...loose. Feel the relaxation. Take a slow, deep breath. Once again with your entire body. Tight...loose. Every muscle in your body is warm and relaxed. Feel the difference between the states of tension and relaxation in your entire body. Take a slow, deep breath.

Now do a mental check list to make sure that every muscle is relaxed. Your feet are relaxed, calves, thighs, buttocks, stomach, back, chest, arms, shoulders, neck, and face. Every muscle in your body is completely relaxed.

Slow pace of match. A common side effect of overintensity is that play-ers tend to speed up the tempo of the match. They rush between points almost as if they want to get the match over with as soon as possible. So, to lower your intensity, slow your pace between points. In my study of players, I've found that few if any use the full 25 seconds they're allowed between points by USTA rules. Simply slowing your pace and giving yourself time to slow your breathing and relax your muscles will help you lower your intensity to its prime level.

Process focus. One of the primary causes of overintensity is focusing on the outcome of the match. If you're worried about whether you will win or lose, you're bound to get nervous. The prospect of losing is threatening, so that will make you anxious. The thought of winning, especially if it's against an opponent you have never defeated before, can also be anxiety provoking because it may be unfamiliar or unexpected to you.

To reduce the anxiety caused by an outcome focus, redirect your focus onto the process. Ask yourself, what do I need to do to play my best ten-nis? This process focus can include paying attention to your technique or tactics. Or it might involve focusing on mental skills such as positive thinking or the psych-down strategies I am currently describing. You can also shift your focus onto your breathing which will take your mind off of the outcome and will directly relax your body by providing more oxygen to your system.

A process focus takes your mind off things that cause your over-inten-sity and shifts your focus onto things that will reduce your anxiety, build your confidence, and give you a greater sense of control over your tennis (to be discussed further in Chapter Six).

Keywords. Another focusing technique for lowering your intensity is to use what I call intensity keywords. These words act as reminders of what you need to do with your intensity to play your best (see Intensity Keywords on page 84). Keywords are especially important in the heat of a tight match when you can get so wrapped up in the pressure that you for-get to do the things you need to do in order to play your best. By saying the keyword between points, you'll be reminded to use the psych-down techniques when your intensity starts to go up. I also recommend that you write one or two keywords on a piece of tape which you then put on your racquet. Looking at your racquet acts as a further reminder to follow the keyword and lower your intensity.

INTENSITY KEYWORDS

Directions: A variety of intensity keywords have been provided below. In the space at the bottom, identify other intensity keywords that you can use.

Psych-Down	**Psych-Up**
Breathe	Go For It
Loose	Charge
Relax	Attack
Calm	Positive
Easy	Hustle
Process	Hit Out
Trust	Commit

Music. Music is one of the most common tools athletes in many sports including tennis use to control their intensity. We all know that music has a profound physical and emotional impact on us. Music has the ability to make us happy, sad, inspired, and motivated. Music can also excite or relax us. Many pros listen to music before matches to help them reach their prime intensity.

Music is beneficial in several ways. It has a direct effect on you physically. Calming music slows your breathing and relaxes your muscles. Simply put, it makes you feel good. Mentally, it makes you feel positive and motivated. It also generates positive emotions such as joy and contentment. Finally, calming music takes your mind off aspects of the match that may cause doubt or anxiety. The overall sensation of listening to relaxing music is a generalized sense of peace and well-being.

Smile. The last technique for lowering intensity is one of the strangest and most effective I've ever come across. A few years ago, I was working with a young pro who was having a terrible practice session. She wasn't hitting the ball well and her coach was getting frustrated with her. She approached me during a water break feeling angry and frustrated, and her body was in knots. She asked me what she could do. I didn't have a good answer until an idea just popped into my head. I told her to smile. She said, I don't want to smile. I told her to smile. She said she was not happy and didn't want to smile. I told her again to smile. This time, just to get me off her back, she did smile. I told her to hold the smile. During the next two minutes there was an amazing transformation. As she stood there with the smile on her face, the tension began to drain out of her body. Her breathing became slow and deep. She said that she was feeling better. In a short time, she was looking more relaxed and happier. She went back on court, her hitting improved, and she played well during the remainder of the practice session.

Her response was so dramatic that I wanted to learn how such a change could occur. When I returned to my office, I looked at the research related to smiling and learned two things. First, as we grow up, we become conditioned to the positive effects of smiling. In other words, we learn that when we smile, it means we're happy and life is good. Second, there's been some fascinating research looking at the effects of smiling on our brain chemistry. What this research has found is that when we smile, it releases brain chemicals called endorphines which have an actual physiologically relaxing effect.

> *"I learned a long time ago that one way to maximize potential for performance is to be calm in my mind and body."*
>
> Former NFL quarterback
> Brian Sipe

Psych-Up Techniques

Though less common, letdowns in intensity can also cause your level of play to decline. A decrease in intensity causes all the things that enable you to play well, for example, to build a 5-1 first set lead, to disappear. Physically, you no longer have the blood flow, oxygen, and adrenaline necessary for the strength, agility, and stamina you need to play your best. Mentally, you lose the motivation and focus that enables you to play well. Just like psych-down techniques when your intensity is too high, you can use psych-up techniques to raise your intensity when it drops.

Intense breathing. Just as deep breathing can reduce intensity, intense breathing can increase it. If you find your intensity dropping, several hard exhales can take your body and your mind to a more intense level. It's a useful practice before a return of serve, where quick reactions are important, to take two intense breaths. In fact, I encourage you to make intense breathing a part of your tennis routine when you're returning serve (to be discussed further in Chapter Nine).

Move your body. Remember that intensity is, most basically, physiological activity. The most direct way to increase intensity is with physical action. In other words, move. Walk or run around, jump up and down. Anything to get your heart pumping and your body going.

Two players who use this technique well are Patrick Rafter and Arantxa Sanchez-Vicario. During a match, both are in constant motion between points and bouncing up and down before return of serve. This activity assists them in maintaining a level of intensity that will allow them to play their best.

High-energy self-talk. One of the main causes of drops in intensity is letdown thoughts. Thinking to yourself, "I've got this match won," "The set is over," or "I can't win this match," will all result in your intensity decreasing. When this happens, you can be sure your game will decline too. When you start to have these thoughts, you need to replace them with high-energy self-talk. Self-talk such as "Keep attacking," "Close it out," and "Stay pumped" will keep you motivated and focused, and your body will respond with more intensity.

Intensity keywords. Just as you can use keywords to lower intensity, they can also be used to counter letdowns and to psych yourself up (see Intensity Keywords on page 84). Saying intensity keywords such as "Charge" and "Hustle" with conviction and energy will raise your intensity and generate positive thoughts and emotions that will enable you to play your best tennis.

High-energy body language. It's difficult using high-energy self-talk and intensity keywords without also having high-energy body language. Pumping your fist or slapping your thigh will also get you fired up and will increase your intensity. Pros like Boris Becker and Conchita Martinez are excellent examples of how high-energy body language can be used to increase intensity.

Music. The value of music has already been described above. Music can also be used to raise your intensity and get you psyched up and motivated. Choose high-energy music that makes you feel good and gets you fired up.

"I like to fire up, to feel the adrenaline flowing; that's when I play my best."

Chris Evert

Key Match Situations

There are common match situations in which you can expect that your intensity will shift away from prime intensity. If you can identify these situations when they occur, you can more quickly take steps to prevent a change in intensity that may hurt your performance. These match situations usually relate to when you're either ahead or behind in a match, or the match is on the line.

Overintensity is most common in pressure situations such as tie-breaks or having to hold serve to stay in the match. Anytime you believe that you must win a point or a game, your intensity will probably rise beyond your prime intensity. Underintensity is seen most often in match situations where you believe that you have the match won, for example, if you're up 40-love in a game, up two breaks in a set, or are serving for the match.

There is not, however, a consistent pattern in how intensity will change for all players. Players in the same match situation can experience different changes in intensity. For example, one player who's serving for the match may have an increase in intensity and feel very nervous because she's never defeated her opponent before and doesn't totally believe that she can. While another player in the same situation might have a decrease in intensity and feel a letdown because she's already mentally in the locker room thinking about her next match. You have to figure out how you typically react and then use the psych-up and psych-down techniques to achieve and maintain prime intensity.

"All pressure is self-inflicted. It's what you make of it, how you let it rub off on you."

Olympic track & field champion Sebastian Coe

Chapter 6

Focus

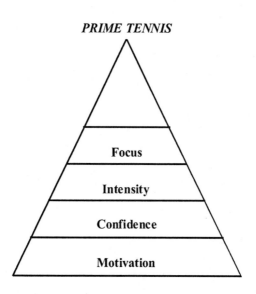

PRIME TENNIS

Focus

Intensity

Confidence

Motivation

Focus is the most misunderstood mental factor among players. Most players think of focus as concentrating on one thing for a long time. In fact, a number of years ago, former Australian Open champion Hana Mandlikova said that she improved her game by staring at a tennis ball for ten minutes a day. But focusing in tennis is much more complex than that. To play Prime Tennis, you have to focus on many different things including the ball, your opponent, the score, technique, tactics, weather, and court conditions.

Let me introduce a term, attentional field, and then I'll define focus for you. Attentional field is everything inside of you, such as thoughts, emotions, and physical responses, and everything outside of you, including sights and sounds, on which you could focus. Focus is the ability to attend to internal and external cues in your attentional field.

Prime focus involves focusing only on performance-relevant cues in your attentional field. In other words, only focusing on cues that help you play your best. Performance-relevant cues include the ball, where you are on the court, your opponent's position on the court, the score, and tactics for the next point. Prime focus gives you the ability to adjust your focus internally and externally as needed. These shifts in focus can be directed toward technique, tactics, or mental areas that impact your tennis.

For example, before you serve, you may focus internally to assess the game situation and what will be the best service tactic. You may then focus on a technical cue that will help you execute the desired serve. Having chosen the type of serve you will make, you turn your focus outward to see where your opponent is preparing to return serve and focus on the area in which you intend to serve the ball.

Poor focus involves focusing on performance-irrelevant cues in your attentional field. That is, focusing on cues that will hurt your tennis. There are two types of harmful cues. Interfering cues are those that will directly hurt your tennis such as negative thoughts, anxiety, and concern over who your next opponent will be if you win. Irrelevant cues are those that simply distract you from an effective focus including what's happening on the next court and what you'll have for dinner tonight.

"What do I mean by concentration? I mean focusing totally on the business at hand and commanding your body to do exactly what you want it to do."

Golfing great Arnold Palmer

Focus Styles

One of the most important developments I've made in my work in recent years is in understanding the importance of identifying players' focus styles. A focus style is a preference for paying attention to certain cues. Players tend to be more comfortable focusing on some cues and avoid or don't pay attention to other cues. Every player has a dominant style that impacts all aspects of their tennis. This dominant style will surface most noticeably when they're under pressure. The two types of focus styles are internal and external.

Internal focus style. Players with an internal focus style play best when they're totally and consistently focused on their tennis during a practice session or a match. They need to keep their focus narrow, thinking only about their tennis. These players tend to be easily distracted by activity in their immediate surroundings. If they broaden their focus and take their mind off their tennis, for example, if they look around to nearby courts during a match or talk about nontennis topics with their coach during a practice, they'll become distracted and will have trouble narrowing their focus back onto their tennis. Pros with an internal focus style include Pete Sampras and Lindsay Davenport.

External focus style. Players with an external focus style play best when they only focus on their tennis when they're about to begin a drill in practice or begin a point in a match. At all other times, they broaden their focus and take their mind off their tennis. These players have a tendency to think too much and become negative and critical. This overly narrow focus causes them to lose confidence and experience overintensity. For these players, it's essential that they take their focus away from their tennis when they're not actually playing.

External focus style runs counter to beliefs held by many coaches. They think that if players are not totally focused on their tennis, then they're not serious about it and they won't play their best. Yet, for players with an external focus style, they don't want to think too much or be too serious because this causes them to be negative and critical. They'll play their best when they're not thinking too much about their tennis and they simply allow their natural abilities to emerge on their own. Pros with an external focus style include Andre Agassi and Martina Hingis.

"I've never been the type of player who responds well to a lot of thinking."

Andre Agassi

Identifying Your Focus Style

With this understanding, you need to identify what is your focus style. Are you a player who needs to keep your mind on your tennis constantly in order for you to play well? Or are you someone who thinks too much and needs to keep your mind off your tennis until its time to play?

Recall past matches and practices when you've played well. Were you totally focused on your tennis or were you keeping your mind off your game? Also, recall past matches and practices when you've played poorly. Were you thinking too much or were you distracted by things going on around you? If you're like most players, a pattern will emerge in which you tend to play best when you focus one way and you play poorly when you focus another way.

Understanding your focus style is essential for you to be able to manage it effectively. This process involves knowing how you focus best and actively focusing in a way that is consistent with your focus style. This ability to manage your focus style well is most important in pressure match situations. There is a tendency for players under pressure to revert back to a focus style that will interfere rather than help their tennis. For example, if you're someone who plays best with an external focus style, you may find yourself turning your focus inward when the pressure is on. You may start to think too much and become negative and critical.

When you start to lose your prime focus style under pressure, you must become aware that you're moving away from it and that you need to take steps to redirect your focus back to the style that works best for you. Continuing the previous example, when you realize that you're focusing internally too much, you should actively turn your focus outward by looking around and taking your mind off your tennis.

"When I'm getting ready for a fight, I like to focus on what I have to do, and talking about it beforehand won't get the job done."

Former boxing great
Tommy Hearns

Mag-Lite® Focus

I've developed a useful tool to help you understand your focus style and to develop focus control. A Mag-Lite® is a flashlight whose beam can be adjusted to illuminate a wide area or to brighten a narrow area. Your focus can be thought of as a Mag-Lite® beam you project that illuminates on what you want to focus.

Players with an internal focus style want to keep their Mag-Lite® beam narrow at all times, only illuminating tennis-related things during practice or matches. If you have an internal focus style, your goal is to stay focused on necessary training or match cues and to block out unnecessary external distractions. To accomplish this, narrow your Mag-Lite® beam by keeping your eyes within the confines of the court and avoid talking to others. Focus on important tennis cues, for example, the proper technique for the next drill or your intensity for the next point. Pros with an internal focus style, like Monica Seles, will, for example, look at and straighten their strings between points.

Players with an external focus style want to widen their Mag-Lite® beam between drills and points to take their mind off their tennis, then narrow their beam shortly before they begin the next drill or point. If you have an external focus style, your goal is to direct your focus off your tennis between drills in practice and between points in matches. To do this, when you're not actually hitting balls, whether in practice or matches, widen your Mag-Lite® beam by looking around you and talking to your coach or other players. This will keep you from thinking too much and becoming negative and critical. Pros with an external focus style, like Goran Ivanisevic, will, for example, look into the stands and talk to fans between points. Shortly before you begin the next drill in practice or next point in a match, narrow your Mag-Lite® beam, focusing specifically on something that will help you play well.

There are also times when, regardless of your focus styles, you'll need to narrow or widen your Mag-Lite® beam. For example, you will want to broaden your beam in a doubles match to identify your opponents' formation before a serve. Other times, you want to narrow your beam, for instance, when you're deciding whether to serve and volley or stay back on the next point.

"When I'm on the mound, I'm so locked in I don't even see the dugouts. It's just me and the glove. There's no way I can hear what's going on in the bleachers."

Baseball great Roger Clemens

Focus Control

Developing focus control is essential if you're going to ensure that your focus style helps rather than hurts your tennis. There are several steps in the focus control process. First, you have to identify your focus style and understand how it impacts your tennis. Next, you must recognize internal and external cues that help and hurt your tennis. Finally, you have to adjust your focus internally and externally as needed during practice and matches.

The eyes have it. We obtain most of our information about the world through our eyes. The most direct way to control our Mag-Lite® beams is to control our eyes. You can think of your eyes as Mag-Lite® flashlights that you can adjust wide or narrow. If you want to minimize the external distractions during practice or a match, narrow your Mag-Lite® beam by keeping your eyes down and on the court. If you're distracted by something, either look away or turn away from it. If you're not looking at something, it can't distract you.

Conversely, if you find that you're thinking too much or being negative or critical, widen your Mag-Lite® beam by raising your eyes and looking around you. For example, see who's playing on the next court. By looking around, you'll be distracted from your thoughts, you'll be able to clear your mind, and then you can narrow your Mag-Lite® beam in preparation for the next point.

Outcome vs. process focus. Perhaps the greatest obstacle to prime focus is having an outcome focus during a match. Outcome focus involves focusing on the possible results of a match: winning, losing, rankings, or who you might defeat or lose to. I tell players that an outcome focus is the kiss of death in tennis.

Many players believe that by focusing on the outcome, that is, on winning the match, they're more likely to achieve that outcome. What most players don't realize is that having an outcome focus actually hurts performance and makes it less likely that they will win. Every time you shift from a process focus to an outcome focus, your game will decline. This drop in performance occurs for several reasons. First, you're no longer focusing on things that will help you play well. Second, it causes your intensity to move away from prime intensity, either up because you start to get nervous over the possibility of losing, or down because you think you already have the match won.

Players don't understand several key things about outcome focus. The outcome comes after the process has occurred and the match is over. The outcome is totally unrelated to the process of the match. In fact, the result of an outcome focus is usually the exact opposite of the outcome players want, specifically, Prime Tennis and winning the match.

The way to achieve the desired outcome of the match is to focus on the process of the match. Process focus involves focusing on aspects of the match that will enable you to play your best, for example, technique, tactics, intensity, or emotions. If you play your best, you're more likely to win. Lindsay Davenport exemplifies the use of process focus. She is always focused and calm. She is not affected by poor play or by being behind in a match. By maintaining a process focus, she's able to play at a consistently high level and win.

Focus on what you can control. A major focusing problem I see with many players is that they focus on things over which they have no control. Players worry about their opponent, the weather, or their draw. This focus has no value because they can't do anything about those things. This kind of focus hurts performance because it lowers confidence and causes worry and anxiety. It also distracts you from what you need to focus on. The fact is, there's only one thing that you can control, and that is you. For example, your attitude, thoughts, emotions, and intensity. If you focus on those things, you'll be more confident and relaxed, and you'll be better able to focus on what you need to do in order to play your best.

Four P's. I have a general rule you can follow that will help you identify what kinds of things you should focus on in your tennis. I call it the four P's. The first P is *positive*. You should focus on positive things that will help your tennis and avoid negative things that will hurt your tennis. The second P is *process*. As I've just explained, you should focus on what you need to do to play your best. The third P is *present*. You should focus on what you need to do right now to play the next point well. You shouldn't focus on the past because it's out of your control and you can't change it. You also shouldn't focus on the future because it's too far away to do anything about. The only way to control the future is to control the present. The only way to control the present is to focus on it. The last P is *progress*. There's a tendency for many players to compare themselves with other players, seeing others advancing farther than them in tournaments and ahead of them in the rankings. How your opponents perform is outside of your control. What you should focus on is your improvement. Players develop at different rates. A player who is ahead of you now may not even be on the same page as you in a year. What's important is that you see yourself progressing toward the goals you want to achieve.

"I stress working in the here and now. On focusing on the ball you're going to hit, how you're going to hit it and the intensity you're going to hit it with, right here, right now."

Gavin Hopper, coach of
Monica Seles

Focusing vs. Thinking

A mistake many players make is that they equate focusing with thinking. They believe that if they're thinking about, for example, their forehand or coming to the net on a short ball, then they're also focusing on it and it will help their game. However, there is a big difference between players focusing on their tennis and thinking about their tennis. This distinction impacts not only players' ability to concentrate on important aspects of their tennis, but it also affects their motivation, confidence, intensity, and emotions.

Focusing simply involves attending to internal or external cues. This process is impartial, objective, unemotional, and detached from judgment or evaluation. If you make a mistake on something on which you were focusing, you're able to accept it and not be overly disappointed by the failure. In a focusing mode, you're able to use the failure as information to correct the problem and focus better in the future.

In contrast, thinking is connected to your ego-investment in your tennis, that is, how important tennis is to you. Thinking is judgmental and critical. If you miss a shot or play poorly when you're in a thinking mode, it hurts your confidence and causes negative emotions such as frustration and anger. Thinking actually interferes with your ability to focus in a way that will help your tennis and it will cause your game to deteriorate.

> *"For sure, I put more pressure on myself, and everyone expects me to win. Everyone is just waiting to see who is going to beat me next. But I do not have trouble concentrating when it counts."*
>
> Martina Hingis

Playing on Both Sides of the Net

When players do not have full command of their game, they must direct most of their focus to the technical, tactical, and mental aspects of their game with little attention pointed toward their opponent. In other words, they have to mentally play entirely on their side of the net.

This phenomenon occurs because players have not instilled key skills that would enable them to "get out of their heads." Typically, these players have not fully ingrained the technical, tactical, and mental aspects of the game to the point that these skills are fully integrated and automatic.

Much of their focus must be on making sure they do the things that will enable them to play well. For example, they have to remember to come to the net on a short ball or serve to their opponent's backhand in the ad court. These players also lack the confidence in their game to trust their abilities. Without that trust in their game, they must stay inside their head to ensure that they do the right things.

In contrast, Prime Tennis enables players to play "on both sides of the net." This expression means that they're able to project themselves onto the other side of the net and can focus more on their opponent's game and how they can be defeated.

Playing on both sides of the net means that you have confidence in your game. You trust that the technical, tactical, and mental skills and habits you have ingrained will emerge automatically and enable you to play your best. Because of this, you can direct more of your attention to your opponent's game. You can focus on their strengths and weaknesses, identify the type of game they're playing, and devise a plan that will enable you to defeat them.

The ability to play on both sides of the net evolves out of your efforts to achieve Prime Tennis. You must first develop the skills and habits that enable you to play your best tennis. During this process, you must also gain the confidence in your abilities. This belief comes from practice and match experience. As you have success playing your game, you will come to trust your abilities and allow them to emerge automatically.

With a foundation of skills and confidence, you can then intention-ally widen your Mag-Lite® beam and direct your focus toward your opponent. As you're playing, you can ask yourself questions about their game: What is their best shot? What seems to be their most inconsistent shot? What style of play do they rely on? What strategy can I use to neu-tralize their game? Simply by asking these questions, you're taking the first step to playing on both sides of the net. At first, you will have to do this deliberately. In time, though, this skill will also become automatic and every time you walk onto the court, you will naturally play on both sides of the net.

> *"Ninety percent of my game is mental. It's my focus that has gotten me this far."*

Chris Evert

Chapter 7

Emotions

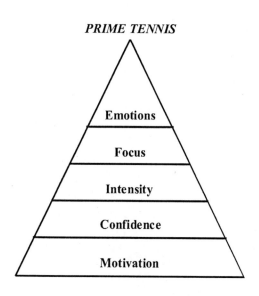

PRIME TENNIS

Emotions

Focus

Intensity

Confidence

Motivation

At the top of the Prime Tennis Pyramid sits emotions. It is closest to the top of the pyramid because emotions will ultimately dictate how you play throughout a match. Emotions during a match can cover the spectrum from excitement and joy to frustration and anger. Emotions are often strong and, most troublesome, they can linger and hurt your game long after you first experience them. Sometimes, very different emotions, for example, joy and anger, can express themselves from one point to the next.

Negative emotions hurt tennis both physically and mentally. They first cause players to lose their prime intensity. With frustration and anger, their intensity goes up and leads to muscle tension, breathing difficulties, and a loss of coordination. It also saps energy and causes players to tire quickly. When players experience despair and helplessness, their intensity drops sharply and they no longer have the physical capabilities to play well.

Negative emotions also hurt mentally. Fundamentally, negative emotions are a response to the perceived threat that players will fail in the situation. Their emotions are telling them that, deep down, they're not confident in their ability to play well and win the match. Their confidence will decline and players will have more negative thoughts to go along with their negative emotions. Also, since negative emotions are so strong, players will have difficulty focusing on what will help them to play well. The negative emotions draw their attention onto all of the negative aspects of their tennis. Finally, negative emotions hurt their motivation to play because it's no longer fun and they just don't feel good.

Emotions come from past experiences in similar situations in the form of beliefs and attitudes players hold about playing and competing. The emotions associated with these beliefs and attitudes are commonly known as the "baggage" people carry from their past. Their perceptions from the past impact their present even though the emotions may not be appropriate or useful in the present situation. One of the most difficult aspects of emotions is that they become habits that cause players to automatically respond with a certain emotional reaction to a particular circumstance even when that emotional response does more harm than good. Martina Hingis' behavior in the 1999 French Open final against Steffi Graf is an example of such destructive behavior. Her frustration and anger, as expressed by pouting, racquet throwing, and, ultimately, her tanking, led to her losing the match and embarrassing herself.

Negative emotions can be provoked by many occurrences during a match including bad calls, cheating, missing an easy shot, making an error at a crucial point in the match, and just playing poorly. All of these events share two common elements that lie at the heart of what causes the negative emotions. Players feel that the path to a goal is being blocked and they don't seem to have control over it. For example, a player is losing to someone and no matter what they try, they can't seem to turn the match around. They're likely to experience frustration and anger initially. These emotions can be helpful at first because they motivate players to fight to clear the path to their goal and regain control of the match. If they're not able to change the course of the match, then players may experience depression and helplessness, in which they accept that they can not win, so they just give up. This emotional reaction is best known as tanking.

Let the Punishment Fit the Crime

In my work with high-level players, I have seen extremely negative emotional reactions to the smallest failures. A missed first serve, a few errors in practice, or the loss of a point in the middle of a match produced frustration and anger that seemed to be out of proportion to the magnitude of the failure. For example, a young pro I worked with would beat herself up emotionally for missing shots in practice. Her level of play would steadily decline and she would feel terrible about her tennis and herself. By the end of the day, she would be battered and bruised by her own emotions. Clearly, the punishment did not fit the crime.

Be sure that your emotions are proportional to what causes them. Ask yourself whether a few missed shots are worth the frustration and anger you might feel and express to yourself. Are you being fair to yourself? When the severity of the punishment exceeds the seriousness of the crime, you have lost perspective on how important tennis is in your life. It might be worth getting frustrated and angry if you didn't get into the college of your choice or you lost your job, but are these strong negative emotions worth feeling over some errors or lost games?

You should also consider whether these emotions help or hurt your tennis. Negative emotions can raise your game at first because they increase your intensity and get you to fight harder. After a short time though, your game begins to decline and it usually spirals downward from there. Negative emotions actually hurt your tennis and keep you from reaching your goals. Why would you allow yourself to experience emotions (frustration, anger, depression) and act in a way (throwing your racquet, choking, tanking) that ensures failure rather than helps you achieve success?

It's okay to be disappointed when you make errors or lose a match. In fact, you should feel that way. It means that you care about the game and want to do better. But when your emotions are stronger and more hurtful than they should be given how minor the crime is (it's just a tennis match) and how often it occurs (you will miss a lot of shots in your tennis life), then you need to look at why your punishment far exceeds the crime you committed.

Look at the pros. Tennis is very important to them because it is their life and livelihood. How upset do they get when they play poorly and lose? Some get very upset. For example, Martina Hingis is well known for her temper tantrums when she is losing. Overall, though, considering how important tennis is to them, most pros handle errors and losses pretty well. In fact, one reason why the top pros are at the top is because they have the ability to control their emotions rather than their emotions controlling them.

"I realized that nobody's perfect. In a way it was such news to me because I'd been in an adult world, and there are such adult expectations to be perfect about everything. And you know, you don't have to be."

Monica Seles

Emotional Threat vs. Emotional Challenge

In recent years, I have found that a simple distinction appears to lie at the heart of the emotional reactions players have to their tennis: threat vs. challenge. At the heart of emotional threat is the perception that winning is all-important and failure is unacceptable. Emotional threat is most often associated with too great an emphasis on winning, results, and rankings. Pressure to win from parents, coaches, and yourself is also common. With these beliefs, it is easy to see why playing tennis would be emotionally threatening.

Emotional threat manifests itself in a negative "emotional chain" in which each link separately and cumulatively makes players feel badly and hurts their tennis. The most common reaction to a threat is the desire to avoid the threat. There is often a loss of motivation to play and compete, especially when the threat of losing is immediate, for example, when a player is behind in a match (think of tanking as a major loss of motivation). Emotional threat also suggests to players that they're incapable of overcoming the situation that is causing the threat, so their confidence is hurt and they're overwhelmed with negative and defeatist thoughts. The threat produces strong negative emotions such as fear, anger, frustration, depression, despair, and helplessness.

The emotional threat also causes anxiety and all of the negative physical symptoms associated with overintensity. The previous links make it nearly impossible to focus effectively because there are so many negative things pulling players' focus away from a useful process focus. All of the previous links in the negative emotional chain ultimately result in very poor play and little enjoyment in the game.

In contrast, emotional challenge is associated with players enjoying the process of tennis regardless of whether they win or lose. The emphasis is on having fun and seeing the competition as exciting and enriching. Tennis, when seen as an emotional challenge, is an experience that is relished and sought out at every opportunity. Thus, emotional challenge is highly motivating, to the point where players love being in pressure situations like tiebreaks and third sets.

Emotional challenge communicates to players that they have the ability to meet the demands of tennis, so they're confident and filled with positive thoughts. Emotional challenge generates many positive emotions such as excitement, joy, and satisfaction. It also stimulates players' bodies to achieve prime intensity, where their bodies are relaxed, energized, and physically capable of playing their best. Players also have the ability to attain prime focus in which they're totally focused on what enables them to play their best tennis. All of these links in the emotional challenge chain lead players to Prime Tennis and great enjoyment in the game.

> *"Emotion is what makes me what I am today. It makes me play bigger than I am."*
>
> Charles Barkley

Emotional Styles

I have found four emotional styles among tennis players. These styles involve characteristic ways in which players respond emotionally to their games. Players with a particular style react in a predictable way any time they find themselves in a threatening situation.

The *seether* feels frustration and anger build slowly during the course of a match. They appear to be in emotional control, but that is only because the negative emotions haven't surfaced yet. They're able to keep the frustration and anger in check as long as the match is mostly going their way. If the match turns or they lose a crucial point, they can explode and lose control emotionally. In most cases, they're not able to reestablish control and end up losing the match. Seethers on the pro tours include Martina Hingis and Yevgeny Kafelnikov.

The *rager* also feels anger and frustration strongly, but it is expressed immediately and openly. For this type of player, showing strong emotions acts as a form of relief. The emotions arise, are expressed, and released. By doing this, the rager is able to maintain a kind of emotional equilibrium. Up to a point, this ongoing emotional outlet helps their tennis by increasing motivation and intensity. However, though these players let the negative emotions out, they do not really let them go. If the match turns against them, the rage builds until it finally engulfs and controls them. At this point, their emotions become their enemies and their game deteriorates. John McEnroe and Goran Ivanisevic are examples of the rager.

The *brooder* also feels strong emotions, but, unlike the seether and the rager, the most common emotions are depression and helplessness. These players tend to dwell on negative experiences, thoughts, and feelings and can be seen as pouting during a match. Brooders are very sensitive to the highs and lows of a match and their emotions tend to mirror its course. If they're playing well and winning, they're fine, but if they play poorly and are losing, the "down" emotions emerge and impact their tennis. They possess a strong defeatist attitude and are best known for their tanking in pressure situations. There are no pros who completely fit this emotional style because someone could not reach such a high level of performance if their dominant emotional style was as a brooder. However, we have seen brooding qualities in players such as Andre Agassi, Conchita Martinez, and Venus Williams.

The *zen master* is the rarest of the emotional styles because they're largely unaffected by threat and negative emotions. As if they're covered in teflon, errors, poor play, and losing seem to slide right off of them. They have the ability to not let pressure situations affect them and they're able to let go of past errors and losses. The zen master rarely shows emotions, either negative or positive, and maintains an consistent demeanor even in the most critical match situations. Zen masters on the pro tour have included Chris Evert, Stefan Edberg, Pete Sampras, and Lindsay Davenport.

What emotional style best describes you? Think back to matches you have played that did not go well. How did you respond emotionally? Were you a seether, rager, brooder, or zen master? It's likely that a pattern of emotional reactions will emerge in your tennis that place you into one of the four emotional styles.

Emotional styles are not easy to change. In fact, there is some evidence that we are born with a particular temperament and we are "hard-wired" that way. If this is true, then it is difficult to change your emotional style. The goal then is not to alter your basic emotional response to the world, but instead to master your emotional style so that it helps rather than hurts your tennis.

"I don't get real emotional. Whatever happens, good or bad, I have to keep the same attitude."

NBA player Mike Bibby

Emotional Master or Victim

Many players believe that they have little control of their emotions and there is nothing they can do to gain control. If their emotions hurt them, they just have to accept it because they can't do anything about it. I call these players *emotional victims*, where their emotions have total control over them, they possess unhealthy and unproductive emotional habits, and their emotions interfere with their happiness and their ability to play well and succeed.

Despite these perceptions, my work has clearly shown that players are capable of becoming *emotional masters*. People can gain control of their emotions. They can develop healthy and productive emotional habits. Their emotions can facilitate their happiness and their ability to succeed.

Emotions are a simple, but not easy, choice. They are a simple choice because if players have the option to feel badly and play poorly or feel good and play well, they will certainly choose the latter option. However, emotions are not an easy choice because past emotional baggage and old emotional habits lead players to respond emotionally in the present in ways that are unhealthy and result in poor performance. The choice comes with awareness of when old emotional habits will arise and choosing a positive emotional response that will lead to good feelings and successful performance.

Responding to Frustration

Frustration is at the heart of every negative emotional reaction. Frustration, in its most basic form, is the emotional reaction to players' efforts toward a goal being thwarted. In other words, if their goal is to play well and win a match, then they may experience frustration if their forehand isn't working or they're down two breaks in the first set.

Frustration can initially be motivating because it pushes players to find a way to remove the obstacles to their goal. If they're unable to turn their game or the match around, then the initial frustration will become more persistent and stronger. Depending on their emotional style, they will either begin to experience anger or despair. If further efforts go unrewarded, then the negative emotions will likely take over and players will get caught in the negative emotional chain I spoke of earlier.

If players can learn to respond positively to frustration when it first occurs, they can prevent other stronger negative emotions from arising and they can stop the negative emotional chain before it starts. Their goal is to react positively to the first indication of negative emotions. This reaction starts with developing a positive attitude about the things that lead to frustration such as errors, poor play, and losing. It means making a shift from an attitude of emotional threat to one of emotional challenge.

Emotional threat is the primary cause of frustration in response to mistakes. Remember that for players who experience emotional threat, failure of any sort is unacceptable. The threat response to frustration causes players to dwell on the past. They continue to worry about missed shots even though there is nothing they can do about the past. These players also play scared because they're afraid of having to face what they perceive as failure. What they don't realize is that this attitude makes it more likely that they will make errors and lose because they put great pressure on themselves to be perfect. Players who play under emotional threat are also emotional victims who feel helpless to do anything about how they feel and can be expected to play their worst on important points.

Yet, failure, in the form of errors and losses, is a normal and inevitable part of tennis. The best players in the world miss shots and lose matches. All players must accept that they will miss a lot of shots and they will also lose matches. These "failures" do not make players failures. Even if players make errors and lose, they can still be good players who hit mostly good shots and win their share of matches. With this emotional challenge attitude, players can unburden themselves of the unrealistic pressure that they must hit every shot well and win every match. With this weight off their shoulders, errors and losses will no longer be a threat and will be less likely to trigger frustration.

Changing this attitude where failure is unacceptable requires that players alter their goal of performance. Most players who have an attitude of emotional threat have perfection as their goal. Players who strive for perfection will continue to experience frustration and the negative emotional chain because they will never achieve the unrealistic and unattainable goal of perfection.

A healthier and more reasonable goal is excellence, which I define as *hitting mostly good shots*. The goal of excellence still sets a high standard of performance, but it also allows the possibility and acceptance of errors and losses. Consider this: If you hit 80% good shots in a match, you will probably win the match. Excellence relieves the pressure of having to hit every shot perfectly and to never miss. Martina Navratilova once told me that early in her career, her perfectionism was the greatest obstacle holding her back. When she made the attitude shift from perfection to excellence her level of play rose dramatically and she became the player we saw dominate women's tennis for almost two decades.

With this emotional challenge attitude in place, you're in a position to take practical steps to counter the frustration you will periodically experience. First, you can learn to identify when frustration usually begins for you. Frustration typically occurs in response to a pattern of missed shots. Perhaps it is after you have double faulted four times or when you have missed three backhands in a row. The next step is to recognize a pattern before frustration arises. If you miss three first serves in row, you know that if you miss a few more, you will become frustrated. It's also important to stay focused on the present rather than dwelling on past mistakes. Having realized that frustration is just around the corner, you can find a solution to the problem so the pattern doesn't continue. For example, you can make a technical or tactical correction that will enable you to get your next first serve in.

Also, realize that you have the opportunity to be an emotional master rather than an emotional victim. As an emotional master, you can choose how you will react to how you're playing. Choose to feel badly and play poorly or feel good and play better. In fact, how quickly you make the choice in response to frustration will determine how long you continue to play poorly and whether you ultimately win or lose the match. The sooner you make the right choice, the sooner you can raise your game and have a chance to win the match.

Emotional Mastery

The process of emotional mastery begins with recognizing the negative emotional reactions that hurt your tennis. When you start to feel negative emotions during a match, be aware of what they are, for instance, frustration, anger, or depression. Then identify what situation caused them, for example, double faulting three times in one game or losing to someone who you believe you should defeat.

After the match, consider what was the underlying cause of the emotions. This might require you to examine your emotional baggage. If the emotions are strong and you find that they present themselves in other parts of your life, you might consider seeking professional help. Such guidance can assist you in better understanding your emotional habits, how they may interfere with many aspects of your life, and how you can learn new emotional responses that will better serve you in your tennis and in your life.

To continue the on-court process of emotional mastery, specify alternative emotional reactions to the situations that commonly trigger negative emotions. For example, instead of throwing your racquet and thinking, "I stink," you could slap your thigh and say, "Come on, better next time." This positive emotional response will help you let go of the past errors, motivate you to play better next point, generate positive emotions that will give you more confidence, and allow you to focus on what will help you raise the level of your game.

Recalling that mental skills like emotional mastery are skills, this positive reaction will not be easy at first because your negative emotional habits are well ingrained. With practice and the realization that you feel better and your game improves with a positive response, you will, in time, retrain your emotions into a positive emotional habit.

Section IV

Prime Tennis Skills

Chapter 8
Prime Tennis Training

As my first law of preparation indicates, matches aren't won on the day of the match, just before the match, or even during the match. Matches are won in training. What you do in training will determine how you play and the ultimate outcome of the match. Training is where the development of Prime Tennis begins. It's the place where all of the physical, technical, tactical, and mental requirements of tennis are established.

Despite this importance, I'm constantly amazed by the poor quality of training in which I see players engage, even at the professional level. I see poor effort, ineffective focus, and little intensity. Yet these players expect to play their best in matches. That's unlikely to happen because they're not engaging in prime training. Prime training involves maintaining the highest level of effort, focus, and intensity consistently throughout a practice session. Without prime training, Prime Tennis will never be achieved.

"Don't mistake activity for training. Practice it the right way."

Basketball coaching legend
John Wooden

Positive Change Formula

Change of any sort, whether physical, technical, tactical, or mental, doesn't occur automatically. There is a three-step process that will enable you to develop your Prime Tennis skills in the quickest and most efficient way possible. I call it the Positive Change Formula (see below). First, you have to become aware of what you're doing incorrectly and how to improve it. Second, you need to control what you want to improve. Finally, you must put in the necessary repetition to ingrain the positive changes fully. Developing your Prime Tennis skills involves an awareness of your physical, technical, tactical, and mental states, taking active steps to control them, and doing sufficient repetition to make the changes automatic. This process produces positive change, which leads to Prime Tennis.

POSITIVE CHANGE FORMULA

Awareness + Control + Repetition = POSITIVE CHANGE

Prime Tennis Training

Too often, I see players walk on the court without any clear idea of what they're doing there. They have nothing in particular they're working on and so they aren't working on anything specific to improve. When this happens, players are not only not improving, they're also making it more difficult to improve because they're ingraining old and ineffective skills, which makes it harder to learn new skills.

Goal and purpose. To prevent this, you need to always train with a goal and a purpose. A goal is some aspect of your game that you want to improve. It might be your serve or your confidence. A purpose is something specific you work on during practice that will enable you to achieve your goal. For example, if your goal is to improve your serve, a purpose might be to work on your toss. Or if your goal is to improve your confidence, your purpose might be to use more positive body language. Every time you walk onto the court to practice, you should have a goal and a purpose. If you don't, you'll be getting better at getting worse.

100% focus and intensity. Another area most players need to work on is their focus and intensity in training. As my eighth law of preparation suggests, players want to train at a level of focus and intensity that will allow them to play their best in matches. Players will play in a match at the level of focus and intensity at which they train. Ideally, players should play at 100% focus and intensity. As I indicated in Chapters Five and Six, players have unique intensity and focus styles in which they play their best. When I talk about 100% focus and intensity, I mean training at or near the level of focus and intensity that allows players to play their best.

Too often I see players training at a level much different than the level at which they want to compete. When they're just hitting or drilling, they may be at 70% focus and intensity. In practice matches, they may up their focus and intensity to 80%. When they get to a match, they want to play at 100%. When they try to do this, one of two things happens. Since they've been training at 70 to 80% focus and intensity, that's what comes out in the match. Or they try to play at 100% focus and intensity, but since they haven't trained at that level, their game actually gets worse rather than better. In either case, the result is that they don't play their best.

Train for adversity. As I suggested in Chapter Four with respect to confidence, an essential skill that you need to develop to play your best is responding positively to adversity. Most players like to train in ideal conditions, but conditions are rarely perfect in matches. Too often in practice, I see players put forth less effort or stop completely when the conditions get too difficult. For example, the sun is in their eyes, the wind is making it hard to hit the ball the way they want, or their practice match opponent is just too frustrating. Players will say it doesn't matter since it's just practice. But players don't realize two things. As my sixth law of preparation states, what you do in practice is what you will do in a match. If you give up in practice when things get too tough, then you're becoming skilled at giving up in the face of adversity. It is often how players respond to adversity that determines who wins the match. The reality is that difficult conditions occur on both sides of the net, so your opponent also has to deal with them. What makes the difference in a match is who responds to the adversity best.

The only way to learn to compete in adverse conditions is to practice in them. This skill comes from accepting that the conditions will interfere with your ability to play your best and also realizing that your opponent must deal with them too. Learning to respond positively to adversity comes from realizing that you probably won't play your best in difficult conditions. You may not realize that you don't have to play well to win a match. You only need to play better than your opponent. By training for adversity, you come to understand the adverse conditions and you learn how to adapt your game to them. By training for adversity, you develop the skills so that your game doesn't deteriorate too much due to the tough conditions.

Responding positively to adversity also comes from being determined not to let the adversity beat you. A part of this is the ability to accept that you will make more errors and to not allow yourself to become frustrated because your game declines. You must stay positive and motivated even when things get tough. Having trained for adversity, when you play a match with adverse conditions, you can say, "I've been training in these conditions. I know what to do to play well. This is no big deal."

One more thing, one more time. One of the greatest lessons I have learned from world-class athletes came from 1972 Olympic skiing gold medallist Bernard Russi. He told me a simple rule that he found enabled him to elevate himself above the other great racers of his time: One more thing, one more time. He assumed that all of his competitors were working hard physically, technically, and mentally. So, every time he came to the end of a workout, he said to himself, "One more thing, one more time." He would then do one more sprint or one more set of weights or take one more training run. By doing one more thing, one more time, he believed he was doing that little bit more than his competitors that would separate himself from them on race day.

The value of mistakes. Perhaps the most frustrating part of tennis is all the mistakes you make as you develop as a player. Most players view mistakes as failure. Players often see errors as a personal attack on their ability as a player and their worth as a person. As I described in Chapter Seven, for many players, making mistakes is unacceptable and a source of frustration and other negative emotions.

Most players don't realize that the best players in the world make errors all the time. What makes great tennis players great is not that they don't hit bad shots, but rather it is the attitude they have about their errors and how they respond to those they do make. Mistakes only mean failure if players don't learn from them and if they keep repeating them.

Mistakes are a natural and necessary part of becoming a better tennis player. Errors really mean that you're becoming more successful because you're moving out of your comfort zone. Mistakes mean you're working to improve. Errors are also valuable information showing you what you need to work on. If you're not making mistakes, you're not pushing yourself to become a better player. They indicate that you're taking risks, going for it, and doing something new. Errors mean success when you learn from them and you stop repeating them.

What is ironic is that most players' attitudes toward errors actually increase the likelihood that the errors will continue. By getting frustrated and discouraged, players are more likely to make more mistakes because they become tentative, doubtful, anxious, and focused on failure. Learning from your errors, and not repeating them, involves knowing how to respond to the mistakes you make. You need to learn to respond in a positive and constructive way.

The goal is to reduce the number of mistakes you make in practice by figuring out how to correct them and ingraining the proper execution. The first step is to identify what you're doing wrong that is causing the error. For example, if you're hitting your first serve into the net, it may be because your toss is too low. Next, you can specify what you need to do to correct the problem. In the case of your serve, you need to toss the ball higher. Then, when you prepare for your next serve, you can focus on the correction, which should solve the problem that's leading to the mistake being repeated.

Get out of your comfort zone. Most players like to stay in their comfort zone. They like to play their game and they get uncomfortable if they try to do anything differently. This approach might make them feel good, but the problem is that they'll never play their best tennis or move up to a new level.

To become your best, you must move out of your comfort zone. This means making changes to your game that will help you in the future. Perhaps you're a baseliner and hate to come to the net. Your comfort zone is staying back. If you want to get better, you need to develop the ability to come to the net on short balls. The risk of moving out of your comfort zone is that you'll make some mistakes at first and might lose some matches. But as you do it more, you become more skilled and familiar with it, until you reach a point at which it's no longer uncomfortable. Before you know it, you've raised your comfort zone and your game to a new level.

The development of Pete Sampras's one-handed backhand is a wonderful example of a player who had the courage to move out of his comfort zone in order to raise his game. When Pete was 15 he was among the best young players in his age group. He also had a two-handed backhand. He and his coaches decided that if he wanted to develop a successful serve-and-volley game and reach the level of play that he has since achieved, he would need a one-handed backhand. For the next year, all he hit were one-handers. During that year, he lost many matches, was defeated by players who he had routinely dominated, and saw his national ranking decline. Pete stuck with his one-handed backhand because he knew it would get him to where he wanted to go, to be the best player in the world.

Never give up. There's a tendency among many players to give up in practice when they're not playing well. They might shorten their drilling because they just can't get a new technique or they tank a practice match because it doesn't really matter. They rationalize giving up by saying that training doesn't really count for anything. My twelve laws of preparation would argue otherwise. Training matters because everything players practice either contributes to or interferes with developing effective skills and habits.

If players give up in practice, they're learning the skill of giving up. If players practice giving up in training, when they play poorly in a match, their learned skill will be to give up. The skill of never giving up is so important because something rather important happens every time players give up: They automatically lose. If players keep fighting, they may not win, but at least they have a chance. Players want to ingrain the skill of playing at 100% and never giving up no matter what happens during a match.

"I never give up in match. However down I am, I fight until the last ball. You can be hopelessly down as long as you win the last point."

Bjorn Borg

Chapter 9

Prime Tennis Routines

Tennis routines are one of the most important aspects of tennis that players can develop to improve their play. The fundamental value of routines is that they ensure total preparation in players' efforts. Routines enable players to be completely physically, technically, tactically, and mentally ready to play their best. I don't know a world-class athlete in any sport who does not use routines in some part of his or her competitive preparations.

Routines are most often used before matches to make sure that when players walk onto the court they're prepared to play their best. They can also be valuable in two other areas. Routines can be developed in training to ensure that players get the most out of their practice time. Routines are also important between points of a match to help players get ready for the next point.

There are a lot of things in tennis that players can't control such as court conditions, weather, the draw, and the opponent. Ultimately, the only thing players can control is themselves. Tennis routines can increase their control over their tennis by enabling players to directly prepare each part of their game that impacts their tennis. Those areas players can control include their equipment (are your racquets strung properly and are your grips in good shape?), their body (are you physically warmed up and are your strokes ready to go?), and their mind (are you at prime focus and intensity?).

Routines also allow players to make their preparation more predictable by knowing they're systematically covering every area that will influence performance. Players can also expect the unexpected. In other words, they can plan for every eventuality that could arise during a tournament. If players can reduce the things that can go wrong and be prepared for those things that do, they'll be better able to stayed focused and relaxed before and during their match.

All of your preparation involves a consistent narrowing of effort, energy, and focus. Each step closer to playing should lead you to that unique state of readiness in which you are physically and mentally ready to play your best. You can think of your preparation as a funnel. Whatever you put into the funnel will dictate what comes out. If you put good preparation into the funnel, what will come out is good tennis. I call this Prime Tennis Funnel.

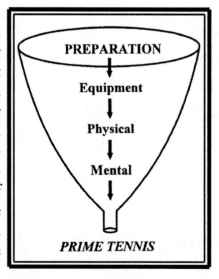

Some sport psychologists use the term, ritual, in place of routine. I don't like this term because it has connotations that go against what routines are trying to accomplish. Remember, the goal of routines is to totally prepare players for training or matches. Everything done in a routine serves a specific and practical function in that readiness process. For example, jumping rope, a hitting warm-up, and a review of tactics for an upcoming match are all essential for total preparation.

In contrast, a ritual is associated with superstitions and is often made up of things that have no practical impact on performance, for instance, wearing lucky socks or following a specific route to the courts. Routines can also be adjusted should the need arise, for example, if you arrive at the courts late, you can shorten your routine and still get prepared. Rituals, though, are rigid and ceremonial. Players can believe that rituals must be done or they will not play well. You control routines, but rituals control you.

"I know when I'm ready to play a great match. I feel my body will respond to my mind no matter what I tell it to do."

Chris Evert

Benefits of Tennis Routines

Tennis routines have many benefits to training and competition. Foremost, they develop consistency in all areas that impact your tennis. By consistently going through your tennis routine, you're training your mind and body to respond the same way regardless of the situation. As my ninth law of preparation suggests, consistent preparation leads to consistent thinking, intensity, focus, emotions, and physical and technical readiness, which will result in Prime Tennis.

At the same time, consistency does not mean rigidity. Routines are flexible. They can be adjusted to different situations that arise, for example, a delay in the start of your match. Flexibility in your routine means you won't be surprised or stressed by changes that occur during your preparations. Flexibility means you'll be better able to play your best in a wider range of playing situations and conditions. Ultimately, the goal of routines in training and matches is to ensure that when you begin play, you're totally physically, technically, tactically, and mentally prepared to play your best.

"To repeat successes of the past, you follow your old program. Don't get fancy; just be consistent."

Former Olympic marathoner
Bill Rodgers

Training Routines

Developing tennis routines should begin in practice. For you to get the most out of your training, you should develop a brief training routine that will ensure that you're totally prepared for every drill. The first step in your training routine is getting your body ready. This involves checking and adjusting your intensity as needed. This might mean taking deep breaths to calm yourself down or using intense breaths to raise your intensity. I recommend that before every drill you move your feet and bounce up and down to get your body going in preparation for the start of the drill. Second, you need to focus on what you want to work on in the drill. If you have an internal focus style, your Mag-Lite® beam should already be narrow and focused on a particular cue. If you have an external focus style, this would be the time to narrow your beam onto the cue. To narrow your focus, you can remind yourself what is the purpose of the drill. Then, you can repeat your key word. At this point as the drill begins, your body and your mind are ready to play Prime Tennis.

Your training routine need only last a few seconds, but will completely prepare you to get the most out of your training. It will also lay the foundation for using tennis routines before and during matches. Remember, for your training routine to become effective, you must use it every time you begin a drill.

"I only play well when I'm prepared. If I don't practice the way I should, then I won't play the way that I know I can."

Ivan Lendl

Pre-Match Routines

The next step in developing effective tennis routines is to create a pre-match routine that is an extended version of the training routine. The goal is the same, to be totally prepared to play your best. The difference is that a pre-match routine will dictate how you play in your upcoming match and it can take up to several hours to complete.

There is no one ideal routine for everyone. Pre-match routines are individual. For every great player, you'll see a different routine, but all will have common elements. You have to decide what exactly to put into your routine and how to structure it. Developing an effective pre-match routine is a progressive process that will take time before you have one that really works for you.

Focus and intensity are two areas that you must consider in developing your pre-match routine. You already know whether you have an internal or external focus style and you know what level of intensity at which you play best. With that in mind, you want to plan your pre-match routine so that when you walk onto the court, you have prime focus and intensity.

Focus needs. The goal in your pre-match routine if you have an internal focus style is to put yourself in a place where there are few external distractions and where you can focus on your pre-match preparation. To maintain that narrow Mag-Lite® beam, you want to go through your pre-match routine away from other people and activities that could distract you. For example, your physical warm-up could be in an isolated part of the tennis facility and your hitting warm-up could be on a far court away from the tournament activity.

An external focus style means that you need to keep your Mag-Lite®
beam wide during your preparations so you can keep your mind off your
match and away from thinking too much. The goal in your pre-match
routine if you have an external focus style is to put yourself in a place
where you're unable to become focused internally and think about the
match. Your pre-match routine should be done where there is enough
activity to draw your focus away from inside your head. To widen the
beam, you want to go through your pre-match routine around people and
activities that can draw your focus outward. For example, you could have
your pre-match meal in the facility's restaurant with other players and you
could sign up for a warm-up court that is at the center of tournament
activity and share it with two other players.

Intensity needs. You'll also want to build your pre-match routine around
your intensity needs. The intensity component of your pre-match routine
should include checking your intensity periodically before the match and
using psych-up or psych-down techniques to adjust it as needed. You'll
need to set aside time in your routine when you can do these techniques.
As you approach your match, you'll want to move closer to your prime
intensity. The short period just before your match should be devoted to a
final check and adjustment of your intensity.

If you play best at a lower level of intensity, you want your pre-match
routine to be done at an easy pace and have plenty of opportunities take
a break to slow down and relax. You'll want to be around people who are
relaxed and low-key as well. If you're around anxious people, they'll make
you nervous too.

If you play best at a higher level of intensity, you want your pre-match
routine to be done at a faster pace with more energy put into the components of your routine. You will want to make sure that you are constantly
doing something. There should be little time during which you are just
standing around and waiting. You'll also want to be around people who
are energetic and outgoing.

Music. Music is a powerful tool you can use to assist in your pre-match preparations. It can help you achieve both prime focus and prime intensity. Music can also positively impact your emotions. Listening to music can help you adjust your Mag-Lite® beam. You can use music as a way of narrowing your Mag-Lite® beam by drawing your focus away from what is happening around you. If you're focused on your music, you won't be paying attention to your surroundings. Music is also a way for you to widen your Mag-Lite® beam by drawing your focus outside of your head. If you're listening to music, you're less likely to be thinking too much about your match.

As I discussed in Chapter Five, music can have a similar impact on your intensity. We all know how powerful music can be. Music has the ability to soothe us or get us fired up. In this way, you can use music to help adjust your intensity. If you need to lower your intensity, you should listen to calming music. If you need to raise your intensity, you should listen to high-energy music.

You can also use music to alter your emotions. Music has the power to inspire us, to excite us, or to make us sad or angry. By playing the right kind of music, you can actively create the emotions you want to play your best. For example, hard rock will energize and motivate you or classical music will make you feel happy and content.

Designing a pre-match routine. The first step in designing a pre-match routine is to make a list of everything you need to do before a match to be prepared. Some of the common elements you should include are meals, review of match tactics, physical warm-up, hitting warm-up, equipment check, and mental preparation. Other more personal things that might go into a pre-match routine include going to the bathroom, changing into your match clothing, and using mental imagery.

Then, decide in what order you want to do the components of your list as you approach the start of your match. In doing this, consider tournament activities that might need to be taken into account. For instance, availability of warm-up courts or a place where you can eat your pre-match meal can influence when you accomplish different parts of your pre-match routine.

Next, specify where each step of your routine can best be completed. You should use your knowledge of tournament sites at which you often play to figure this part out. For example, if you like to be alone before your match, is there a quiet place you can get away from people?

Finally, establish a time frame and a schedule for completing your routine. In other words, how much time do you need to get totally prepared? Some players like to get to the courts only a short time before their matches. Others like to arrive hours before. All of these decisions are personal. You need to find out what works best for you. Use the Personalized Tennis Routine form (see page 131) to assist you in developing your pre-match routine.

Once your pre-match routine is organized, try it out at tournaments. Some things may work and others may not. In time, you'll be able to fine-tune your routine until you find the one that's most comfortable and best prepares you for your matches. Lastly, remember, pre-match routines only have value if they're used consistently. If you use your routine before every match, in a short time, you won't even have to think about doing it. Your pre-match routine will simply be what you do before each match and it will ensure that you are totally prepared to play your best.

"I attach a great deal to mental preparation before a final."

Chris Evert

PERSONALIZED PRE-MATCH ROUTINE

Directions: List the pre-match activities that will help you to totally prepare to play your best.

Early in Day

1.   Physical:

2.   Mental:

At Courts

1.   Physical:

2.   Mental:

Final Preparation

1.   Equipment:

2.   Physical:

3.   Mental:

Match Routines

The last place where routines can be invaluable is between points of a match. Tennis involves a series of short performances. Being well-prepared for the first point is not enough. You must ensure total preparation for every point of the match. One thing that I found that separates the great players from the good ones is their ability to be consistently ready for every point of the match. By being totally prepared for every point, you can be sure that you won't give your opponent "free" points because you weren't ready.

The time between points is essential to consistent match play. What you think, feel, and do between points will often dictate how you play each point. You must take control of the time between points to be sure that you're totally prepared.

I use a four-step match routine called the Four R's. The first R is *rest*. Immediately after the conclusion of the previous point, take several slow, deep breaths and let your muscles relax. This is especially important after a long or demanding point in which you get out of breath. It's also important near the end of a long match in which you're tired and need to recover as much as possible to be ready for the next point. Deep breathing and relaxing also help you center yourself and better prepare you for the next R.

The second R is *regroup*. This phase of the match routine addresses your emotions between points. Particularly when you are not playing well or the match is at a critical juncture, you may feel a variety of emotions such as excitement, frustration, anger, or depression. Regrouping allows you to gain awareness of how your emotions are impacting you and, if they are affecting you negatively, to master them so they help rather than hurt you on the next point. If you are emotional after a point, for example, if you just lost a crucial point and you are frustrated and angry, you should give yourself more time to regroup and let go of the unhealthy emotions. Because of the powerful influence emotions have on your tennis, your ability to "get your act together" emotionally between points may be the most important thing you can do to prepare for the next point.

An important realization that can make regrouping easier is that points in a match are not directly related to each other. In other words, the chances of winning the next point are in no way associated with whether you won the last point. For example, hitting a forehand into the net on the last point has no direct bearing on how you will play on the next point.

One thing that connects points are the emotions attached to the last point. If you're frustrated and angry about the last point, you increase your chances of losing the next point because negative emotions usually interfere with good tennis. In contrast, if you have positive emotions about the last point, you increase your chances of winning the next point because positive emotions will make you more motivated and confident which, in turn, will enable you to play better. Using the time to regroup will enable you to let go of and replace the negative emotions with positive ones, thereby increasing your chances of winning the next point by raising the level of your game.

The third R is *refocus*. There can be a tendency during matches, especially in pressure situations, to focus on the last point or the outcome of the match. This is a form of outcome focus in which you're focusing on whether you won or lost the last point or the possible result at the end of the match. When this happens, you need to return to a process focus on the next point. During the refocus phase of the tennis routine, you should first evaluate your present situation, for example, the score, how you've been playing, and tactics. Then, focus on what you need to do to play the next point well. Your focus may be technical, like adjusting your toss, tactical, for example, hitting more angles, or mental, such as being more aggressive on your shots. The important thing is to begin the next point with a clear focus on what you want to do to play your best.

The fourth R is *recharge*. If your body is not prepared, you won't be able to play your best tennis. Just prior to beginning the point, you should check and adjust your intensity. If you need to lower your intensity, you should slow your pace, take deep breaths, and relax your muscles. If you need to raise your intensity, you should increase your pace, take some short, intense breaths, and jump up and down.

A similar process can occur on changeovers. Changeovers give you an extended period in which you can prepare yourself for the next game. They also give you the opportunity to focus on one phase of the four R's that needs special attention. For example, if you're struggling emotionally because you played poorly and your serve was broken in the last game, you can use the changeover to let go of the negative emotions, find a solution for why you played so poorly, and reestablish some positive emotions you can use to get back in the match.

Chapter 10

Prime Tennis Imagery

Tennis imagery is one of the most powerful tools you can use to improve your tennis. It's used by virtually all great tennis players and there is considerable scientific research supporting its value. This research indicates that using tennis imagery alone produces gains in performance. More importantly, combining actual tennis practice with tennis imagery results in more improvement than practice alone.

Tennis imagery is so beneficial because it impacts every contributor to Prime Tennis. It improves every part of the Prime Tennis pyramid. Tennis imagery increases motivation by seeing and feeling yourself working hard and reaching your goals. It builds confidence by seeing and feeling yourself perform well and succeed. Tennis imagery improves intensity by allowing you to imagine experiencing pressure and using psych-up or psych-down techniques to control it. It enhances focus by identifying important cues and letting you rehearse prime focus. Finally, tennis imagery enables you to generate positive emotions in response to seeing and feeling yourself play your best.

Tennis imagery also improves technical, tactical, and competitive development. It ingrains the image and feeling of correct technique and provides imagined repetition of proper execution. Tennis imagery also enables you to further learn sound tactics and instill effective competitive skills, habits, and routines. Finally, it ingrains the image and feeling of playing your best tennis.

Tennis imagery can be used in several settings that will help you play Prime Tennis. On-court, you can use it to facilitate your technical development and improve the quality of your training. Off-court, you can use tennis imagery to complement your on-court practice and as part of your pre-match routine.

> *"Of all our faculties the most important one is our ability to imagine."*
>
> Wilt Chamberlain

Tennis Imagery is a Skill

It's important to understand that tennis imagery is a skill, just like a technical skill, that develops with practice. Few players have perfect tennis imagery when they first use it. It's common for players who haven't used tennis imagery before to struggle with it at first. This discourages them and leads them to believe that tennis imagery can't be beneficial. If players put in the time and effort, their tennis imagery will improve and it will become a valuable tool for them.

The first thing you want to do is assess your imagery abilities. To do this, complete the Tennis Imagery Profile (see page 138). It will give a graphic representation of your tennis imagery strengths and areas in need of improvement. Using this information, you can emphasize and strengthen the areas in need of work in your tennis imagery program. The next section will describe each factor in more detail and provide exercises to improve each imagery area.

"I'd try to create an instant replay on the inside of my eyelids. Usually I'd catch only part of the particular move the first time I tried this. But the next time I saw the move I'd catch a little more of it, so that soon I could call up a complete picture."

Basketball great Bill Russell

Tennis Imagery Factors

Perspective—Internal imagery (from inside your body looking out) or external imagery (from outside your body like watching yourself on video) or both. (1-all internal; 5-both; 10-all external)

Control—Control of your images as you play (e.g., play well with an accurate image of how you play or difficulty imagining how you play or making errors in your imagery). (1-no control; 10-total control)

Visual—How clearly you see yourself playing (e.g., see ball, court, and self). (1-unclear; 10-clear)

Auditory—How clearly you hear sounds associated with tennis (e.g., ball hitting the racquet, shoes against court). (1-unclear; 10-clear)

Physical feelings—How clearly you feel yourself playing (e.g., muscles working, contact of the ball, court under your feet). (1-unclear; 10-clear)

Thoughts—How well you are able to reproduce the thoughts that you have when you are playing (e.g., about technique, tactics, positive or negative). (1-no thoughts; 10-usual thoughts)

Emotions—How well you are able to reproduce the emotions that you feel when you are playing (e.g., excitement, frustration, anger, depression). (1-no emotions; 10-strong emotions)

Total image—How well you are able to accurately reproduce the playing experience (e.g., all of the senses, thoughts, emotions, and physical feelings) (1-poor reproduction; 10-exact reproduction)

Speed—Your ability to speed up or slow down your imagery. (1-not all; 10-easily)

TENNIS IMAGERY PROFILE

Name _____   **Date** _____

Directions: Nine factors that are important for tennis imagery are identified in the profile below. Before rating yourself on each factor, close your eyes and imagine playing for 30 seconds, paying attention to a particular factor. Indicate how you perceive yourself on the 1-10 scale for each factor by drawing a line at that rating number and shading in the area toward the center of the profile. Except for Perspective, a score below a <u>7</u> indicates an area in need of improvement.

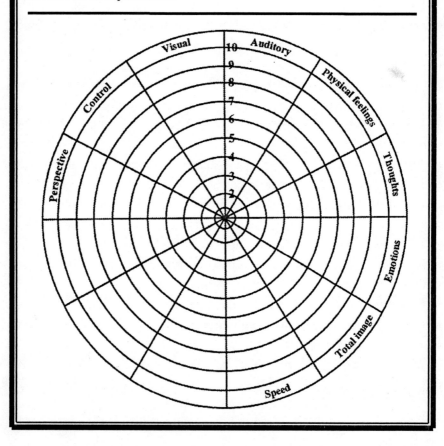

Maximizing Tennis Imagery

There are seven factors that will impact the quality of your tennis imagery: perspective, control, multiple sense, thoughts, emotions, total image, and speed. Each of these areas can be developed with practice.

Imagery perspective. Imagery perspective refers to where the "imagery camera" is when you do tennis imagery. You will use one of two perspectives. The internal perspective involves seeing yourself from inside your body looking out, as if you were actually playing. The imagery camera is inside your head looking out through your eyes. The external perspective involves seeing yourself from outside your body like on video. The imagery camera follows your performance from the outside.

Research indicates that one perspective is not better than the other. Rather, most people have a dominant perspective with which they're most comfortable. There are also some people who are equally adept at both perspectives. You should use the perspective that's most natural for you and then experiment with the other perspective to see if it helps you in a different way.

Try this exercise. Imagine yourself in four rallies in which you hit groundstrokes for 30 seconds. The first two times use your dominant perspective. The next two times use the other perspective. You may find that only one perspective works for you or you may find that you can use either perspective equally well. In either case, for the time being, rely on the perspective that comes most naturally to you.

Control. Have you ever been doing tennis imagery and you keep making errors, for example, you keep hitting balls into the net? This problem relates to imagery control, which is how well you're able to imagine what you want to imagine. It's not uncommon for players new to tennis imagery to keep missing shots in their imagery. This can be frustrating because if you can't imagine good tennis in your head, you're probably going to have a difficult time playing good tennis on the court.

You may find that the amount of imagery control you have depends on which shot you are hitting. In general, you will have the most imagery control over the shots at which you are most skilled and most confident and you will have the least control over shots at which you aren't very good and lack confidence. For example, if your volley game is weak and you don't have much faith in it, you will probably find that you miss a lot of volleys in your tennis imagery.

Imagery control is a skill that develops with practice. If mistakes occur in your imagery, you shouldn't just let them go by. If you do, you'll ingrain the negative image and feeling which will hurt your tennis. Instead, when you make errors in your imagery, immediately rewind the "imagery video" and edit it. That is, rerun the imagery video until you do it correctly.

Try this exercise. Imagine yourself playing five times for 30 seconds. In each segment, if you make a mistake, rewind and edit your imagery until you get it right. I've sometimes found it difficult for players to edit their imagery when they imagine themselves playing at full speed. It can be helpful when they're having difficulty controlling their imagery to slow their imagery down, in which they see and feel themselves playing in slow motion. This technique seems to enable players to have greater control of their imagery. As they gain better control of their imagery in slow motion, they can progressively increase the speed of their imagery while maintaining good control until they're able to play well at "real time" speed.

Multiple senses. You may have noticed that I use the word imagery rather than visualization to describe this technique. This is because visualization places too much emphasis on its visual component. Good tennis imagery is more than just visual. The best imagery involves the multi-sensory reproduction of actual tennis. You should see, hear, and feel your tennis imagery.

Visual imagery involves how clearly you see yourself playing. Ideally, your visual images should be as clear as if you are actually playing. It may be, though, that your images are blurry or you can't see yourself at all.

In order to imagine yourself playing, you must know what you look like as a player. If you can't produce an accurate image of how you hit the ball, you will probably imagine yourself playing like someone you practice with or like a pro. In either case, the images will not help you because they will be inconsistent with how you actually play.

Try this exercise. Watch yourself playing on video, then immediately close your eyes and reproduce the video images. As the visual image of how you play becomes more clear, put away the video for a while and repeat the accurate visual images of your tennis. If the image starts to fade, return to the video until you're able to see yourself playing consistently. This exercise will help you ingrain an accurate image of how you play.

Vivid auditory images are important because we use sounds during a match to help us judge many aspects of the game. The sound of the ball coming off the racquet tells you whether the ball was hit flat or with spin. There is the sound of your shoes against the court as you move. Labored breathing by opponents lets you know that they are getting tired. Negative talk from opponents tells you that they're becoming discouraged.

Try this exercise. Imagine playing three times for 30 seconds. Each time, focus on a different sound associated with a tennis match. Once you're able to do this consistently, put all of the sounds together and hear the various sounds in one sequence of tennis imagery.

I believe that the most powerful part of tennis imagery is feeling it in your body. That's how you really ingrain new technical and mental skills and habits. A useful way to increase the feeling in your tennis imagery is to combine imagined and real sensations. Imagine yourself playing and move your body with the imagined tennis. By integrating the imagined sensations with the actual physical feelings, you can improve the value of tennis imagery even more.

Try this exercise. Imagine playing two times for 30 seconds. Each time, focus on feeling your muscles and the physical movements. Then, imagine playing two more times focusing on the feeling, but this time, move your body with the imagery to simulate the actual movement, for example, a groundstroke. By combining the imagined feelings with the actual physical feelings, you'll further enhance the quality of your tennis imagery and increase its benefits.

Thoughts. What you think during a match often dictates your intensity, emotions, and how you play. Tennis imagery gives you the ability to learn new and better ways of thinking during matches. You can generate match situations in your imagery in which you have displayed negative self-talk and body language. Drawing on the techniques described in Chapter Four, you can replace the negative self-talk and body language with positive expressions that will help you achieve Prime Tennis. Using tennis imagery in this way enables you to gain the added repetition of positive thinking that will further ingrain new positive thinking skills.

Try this exercise. Imagine yourself in a match situation in which you have negative self-talk and body language, for example, your serve was just broken to go down 4-5. Allow yourself to experience the negative thoughts and body language, then imagine yourself replacing the negatives with positive expressions using thought-stopping, positive keywords, and positive body language. Then, imagine yourself playing well and breaking back to even the set at 5-5.

Emotions. Emotions play an important role in your ability to achieve Prime Tennis. Incorporating them into tennis imagery can be a valuable way to ingrain positive emotions into your tennis. Much like in actual matches, imagining scenarios that have in the past evoked negative emotions gives you the opportunity to respond to them in an emotionally different way.

Try this exercise. Imagine yourself in a match situation in which you feel negative emotions, for example, you get frustrated when you miss every first serve in a game. Allow yourself to experience the frustration and then project yourself to your next service game and replace the negative emotions with positive ones that will help you get your first serve in.

Total image. Another key aspect of tennis imagery is being able to imagine the total performance. The most effective imagery reproduces every aspect of the actual performance. In your tennis imagery, you should duplicate the sights, sounds, physical sensations, thoughts, and emotions that you would experience during an actual match.

Try this exercise to improve your ability to recreate the total perform-ance. Imagine yourself playing five times for 30 seconds. In each segment, choose a different aspect of the performance to focus on, for example, visual, auditory, physical feeling, thoughts, and emotions. Emphasize experiencing that part of the playing experience. Then, imagine playing five more times. In these performances, combine all the aspects of tennis imagery and imagine the total performance. The more you can exactly reproduce the actual playing experience, the more you'll get from your tennis imagery.

Speed. The ability to adjust the speed of your imagery will enable you to use tennis imagery to improve different aspects of your game. Slow motion is effective for focusing on technique. During actual practice, it's difficult to work on technique at full speed. Instead, you begin technical change at slow speed under easy conditions. The same thing works for tennis imagery. When you first start to work on technique in your imagery, slow the imagery video down, frame by frame if necessary, to see yourself executing the skill correctly. Then slowly increase the speed of your imagery to "real time" until you're able to execute the technique at full speed.

You can use high-speed tennis imagery to improve your speed and reac-tions. Just as in actual training, thoughts and external distractions can interfere with play. It can be difficult to maintain focus and rely on your reactions to play well. Similarly, in imagery, thoughts can intrude and can hurt focus and the imagined performance. Use fast motion imagery to develop better focus and to improve your reactions. Speed up your tennis imagery so you don't have time to be distracted. High-speed imagery reduces thinking, primes reactions, and hones automatic performance.

Try this exercise. Choose a technique you're working on in your tennis. Imagine performing the technique six times. The first two times, slow down the imagery so you can really focus on doing it correctly. If you can do the technique properly at slow speed, increase the speed to a moderate rate. If you can do the technique correctly at a moderate speed, increase the imagery to full speed. You know you have the technique ingrained in your mind and body when you can do it correctly at high speed.

"When I am running hard, I visualize myself running my goal race. I also visualize myself from an outsider's view. I visualize myself finishing the race with that elated feeling and running a really great time."

Runner Jerry Lawson

Tennis Imagery for Prime Training

There are several places you can incorporate tennis imagery into your training. Just before you begin a drill, instead of thinking about what you want to work on, see and feel yourself doing it with tennis imagery. Close your eyes and briefly imagine how you want to perform the drill. This will increase your focus on the purpose of the drill and give you a positive image and feeling that will help its execution.

You can also use tennis imagery when you've finished a drill. If you just had a great drill in which you hit the ball well, the most important thing you want to do is remember the image and feeling. So right after the drill, close your eyes and replay the drill with tennis imagery. This will ingrain the positive image and feeling.

If you just had a poor drill in which you made errors, the dominant feeling and image is negative. The last thing you want to do is remember it. Yet, that is the image and feeling in your mind and body, and it is what will come out when you begin your next drill. You need to flush out the negative image and feeling. Right after the drill, edit your tennis imagery, this time performing the drill well. This editing process clears out the negative image and feeling and replaces it with positive ones.

You can also use tennis imagery after your coach or pro has given you instruction. Typically, a coach will give you feedback and then will tell you to think about it before you begin the next drill. But where does thinking occur? In your head. Where does playing occur? In your body. Thinking about instruction doesn't always translate into the body effectively. Tennis imagery acts as a bridge between the thoughts in your mind and the actions in your body. You can use tennis imagery to ingrain the instruction into your mind and body. After your coach gives you instruction, close your eyes and imagine yourself making the correction that you were just told.

Tennis Imagery for Matches

Tennis imagery can be a valuable tool during matches. If you're missing a shot and need to make a correction, instead of thinking about what you need to do to correct it, use tennis imagery. Either between points or on a changeover, close your eyes and imagine yourself hitting the shot the way you want. Be sure to focus on the correction in your imagery and to see and feel yourself doing it properly. Using tennis imagery in this way will give you confidence that you can successfully hit the shot again, generate positive emotions that will make you feel better, and increase your focus on the change. It will also take your mind off of negative thoughts and feelings that may have arisen in response to your poor play.

Tennis imagery can also be used to change strategy during a match. Rather than thinking about a change in tactics, for example, deciding to come in behind short balls, imagine yourself playing that way. This approach allows you to practice your change in strategy before you actually use it.

"I'm visualizing every single part of the downhill course. I want it to be totally rehearsed in my head."

Olympic ski racer
Chad Fleischer

Developing an Off-Court Tennis Imagery Program

An off-court tennis imagery program allows players to systematically address key areas they need to improve in their tennis. Players can use tennis imagery to consistently develop technical, tactical, and mental aspects of their game.

Tennis imagery goals. The first step in developing an off-court tennis imagery program is to set goals. They could be technical, such as improving your down the line backhand, tactical, such as coming to the net behind short balls, mental, such as increasing your confidence or reducing your intensity, or relate to overall performance, such as improving your consistency or being more aggressive. Use the Tennis Imagery Goals form (see page 147) to identify the areas on which you want to work.

TENNIS IMAGERY GOALS

Name _____   Date _____

Directions: In the space below, indicate your goals for your off-court tennis imagery program. Be specific in identifying areas where you want to improve your game.

Technical

      1.

      2.

Tactical

      1.

      2.

Mental

      1.

      2.

Overall Play

      1.

      2.

Tennis imagery ladder. The next step involves creating a tennis imagery performance ladder. You wouldn't begin to change a part of your game in an important match. Rather, you would start off practicing new skills in a practice situation where mistakes don't matter. Similarly, you don't want to begin your tennis imagery program in a big imagined match. Using the Tennis Imagery Ladder form (see page 149), create a ladder of practice and match situations in which you'll be playing. The ladder should start with the least important practice situation and increase up to the most important match in which you will play. For example, a low rung of the Tennis Imagery Ladder could be hitting with a friend and high rung could be playing in your club championships. This ladder enables you to work on areas you've identified in increasingly more demanding situations.

You should begin your tennis imagery program at the lowest rung of the ladder and work your way up until you've reached the highest rung. Don't move up to the next rung until you can play the way you want at the current rung. Once you feel good at a particular rung, stay there for several imagery sessions to reinforce the positive images, thoughts, and feelings.

TENNIS IMAGERY LADDER

Name _____   Date _____

Directions: In the space below, create a ladder of practice and match situations in which you will imagine yourself. The ladder should increase incrementally in terms of importance. Specify the playing situation (e.g., drilling, practice match, or tournament match). Examples are italicized.

Least Important

    1. *(hitting with a friend)*

    2. *(drilling with coach)*

Moderately Important

    3. *(practice match)*

    4. *(early round match)*

Most Important

    5. *(finals of tournament)*

Create tennis imagery scenarios. Once you've established your goals and built your tennis imagery ladder, you're ready to create practice and match scenarios that you will follow in your tennis imagery sessions (see Tennis Imagery Scenarios on page 151). These scenarios are actual practice or match situations in which you can work on your technical, tactical, mental, and performance goals.

Unlike some sports such as figure skating and gymnastics in which competitive performances last, at most, a few minutes, you can not imagine yourself playing an entire match. Instead, you should identify four or five playing situations that are realistic. For example, if one of your goals is to improve your backhand volley, a practice scenario might be to hit four sets of 30 backhand volleys in your tennis imagery. As you move up the tennis imagery ladder, a match scenario might involve imagining four or five game situations in which you come to the net often and hit your backhand volley properly.

TENNIS IMAGERY SCENARIOS

Name _____ **Date** _____

Directions: In the space below, create several practice and match scenarios that you can follow in your off-court tennis imagery sessions as you climb your tennis imagery ladder. These scenarios should provide you with detailed descriptions of what you want to imagine as you work on some part of your game in training and matches.

Practice

Match

Tennis imagery log. Since tennis imagery is not tangible like, for example, weight lifting where you can see how much weight you've lifted, it's useful to keep a log of your tennis imagery sessions. By recording your tennis imagery sessions, you'll be able to see improvement as you make your way up the ladder. Use the Tennis Imagery Log (see page 154) to record relevant aspects of your imagery sessions.

The first piece of information you should record is the *rung* of the tennis imagery ladder. Place a number between one and five to indicate where you are in your climb up the ladder. Rate the *quality* of the imagery session on a 1-10 scale. How clear were the images, how well did you play, how did you feel about the imagery session?

Describe your *performance*, that is, what you worked on and what you actually imagined during the imagery session. For example, you worked on your forehand and you imagined yourself hitting four sets of 30 down the line forehands. Specify the *number of errors* you made in the imagery session. Then indicate what *type of errors* you made most frequently.

Rate the quality of the your *senses* in your imagery session. Assign yourself a 1-10 score for how clear was the visual, auditory, and physical imagery you experienced. Lastly, evaluating the *mental* aspects of your imagery, briefly describe relevant thoughts and emotions you had during your imagery session. The emphasis of this area should be on how positive or negative were your thoughts and emotions.

Practical concerns. It's important that your imagery scenarios are practice or match specific. You shouldn't just imagine yourself playing in a nonspecific location, event, and under undefined conditions. Rather, you should imagine a practice or match scenario in which you play at a particular site, in a specific match, against a identifiable opponent. Also, be sure that the events, locations, conditions, and opponents are appropriate for your level of play. If you're a junior player, you shouldn't imagine yourself playing the finals of Wimbledon against Pete Sampras or Monica Seles.

You should structure your tennis imagery sessions into your daily routine. If you schedule them for the same time every day, you're more likely to remember to do them. Find a quiet, comfortable place where you won't be disturbed. Each session should last no longer than 10 minutes. Do tennis imagery three to four times a week. Like any form of training, if you do it too much, you'll get tired of it. Finally, start your tennis imagery sessions with one of the relaxation procedures that I described in Chapter Five. The deep state of relaxation will help you generate better quality images and it will make you more receptive to the images and feelings you're trying to ingrain.

"I've discovered that numerous performers use the skill of mental rehearsal. They mentally run through important events before they happen."

Psychologist Charles Garfield

TENNIS IMAGERY LOG

Date	LADDER: $\#$ of rung	QUALITY: 1-10	PERFORMANCE: What you imagined	CONTROL: $\#$ & type of errors	SENSES: Visual - Auditory - Physical	MENTAL: Thoughts and emotions

Chapter 11

Prime Match

The result of achieving Prime Tennis is what I call a Prime Match, when you're able to play your best tennis from the start of a match to its conclusion. This is one of the characteristics that differentiates experienced pros from even young pros, and the players at any level who win matches consistently from those who lose them. Prime match players are able to maintain a high level of play throughout a match with few letdowns. I found three distinct stages that determined whether a player could accomplish a prime match.

Prime start. The first stage I call Prime Start. One of the first lessons that emerged from my work with pros was that players could not afford to start slowly. It is not uncommon for players from weekend warriors to juniors to pros to believe that they can settle into the match the first few games then really turn it on. In a sense, this approach is making a fundamental mistake: players are using the beginning of the match as a warm-up. Against a tough opponent in an important match, this will not work. The match is simply not the time to get warmed up.

If you're playing against someone whom you are better than, then you can fall behind and once you get going, you'll be able to catch up and defeat them. However, these matches are not why you're striving to achieve Prime Tennis. The real meaning of playing Prime Tennis is that you're playing an opponent who is as good or better than you in a match that matters to you. Against this player a slow start will be a kiss of death. You will not be able to play your way into the match. If you try this, you will find that you will be down, for example, 2-5 before you know it and your opponent is too good and too tough to let you back into the match.

Having a prime start goes back to many themes I have discussed throughout this book, most notably, being totally prepared to play your best from the very first point. Your ability to experience a prime start depends on whether you're physically, technically, tactically, and mentally ready to play Prime Tennis from the start of the match.

At the heart of this readiness is your pre-match routine. It should ensure that you are completely ready to hit out on the very first ball. There are several key components to making sure this happens. First, you must have a good physical warm-up. If your body is not prepared, you will not be able to have a prime start to the match. Your physical warm-up should include everything necessary to ensure total physical readiness. Common physical warm-up activities include a short run, jumping rope, stretching, and agility and footwork drills. This part of the pre-match routine will also help you move toward your prime intensity.

The next step in your pre-match preparations should be your hitting warm-up. This is a process by which every shot that you will hit in a match is hit repeatedly until you are confident and comfortable. This is an area where I see many players fall short. Most hitting warm-ups I see are unstructured and unfocused, in which players hit a few basic groundstrokes, volleys, and serves, and deem themselves warmed up.

A hitting warm-up that leads to a prime start should be organized and comprehensive. For example, you can start with groundstrokes, hitting them crosscourt and down the line, with different spins and at various speeds. Then, move to volleys and overheads, hitting for depth and angle. Specialty shots like drop shots and lobs should also be warmed up. Next, hit serves on both sides of the court, systematically moving through different locations in the service box and hitting with various speeds and spins. The most neglected shot in pre-match warm-up, the return of service, should be hit, on both the deuce and ad courts, returning to different locations with differing pace and spin. The hitting warm-up should conclude with you playing out some points in which you serve and return.

At the end of the hitting warm-up, you should have hit every shot that you will use in a match. Moreover, the last few shots of each part of the warm-up should be hit with match focus and intensity. This last step enables you to hit your first shot in the match with absolute confidence and comfort.

The final step of the prime start warm-up is to review your strategy for the match, check your equipment (e.g., string, grips, shoe laces), and make the final adjustments to your focus and intensity. When the match begins and you hit your first shot, you can play your game to your fullest ability and ensure that you will be competitive from the very first point.

Prime process. Another place in which players often see a decline in their game is in the middle of the match. It often occurs, for example, at the start of the second set. This decrease in performance is usually in response to winning or losing the previous set. It is caused by a change in focus and intensity from earlier in the match.

It is common after winning the first set to experience a change in focus and a letdown in intensity. Winning the first set can cause overconfidence and the belief that players will win the match. When this thought, "I have the match won," occurs, it signals to the mind and body that they can relax. Focus shifts away from what enabled players to win the first set and their intensity drops so they're no longer physically capable of playing at that winning level in the second set. It can also cause players to change their strategy, "If I just play it safe now, I will win the match." Taylor's Law of Stupidity applies here: if it's working, change it. That is just dumb. If you have something that's working, you should stick with it.

After losing the first set, there can be the tendency to become discouraged and lose confidence. If players think, "I can't win this match now," their focus shifts onto the negative thoughts and feelings and their intensity either drops because they give up or it goes up because it is very threatening for them to think that they will lose.

At the same time, Taylor's Law of Insanity often applies: doing the same thing and expecting different results. Many players don't consider whether they need to change their game at this point in the match. Certainly, in some cases, if players stick with their game, it can come around and it can turn the match in their favor. More often than not, though, players fall behind because their strategy is not working.

At this stage of the match, several things need to be done to achieve prime process. First, you have to consider what you need to do tactically to maintain (if you're winning) or raise (if you're losing) your game. It may be that you should just keep doing what you are doing or you need to figure out what you can do to turn the match around. Then, you have to take active steps to reestablish prime focus. This usually involves returning to a process focus in which you focus on what you need to do to play well. Finally, you need to use psych-up or psych-down techniques to reach your prime intensity.

Prime finish. This final step in a prime match involves playing your best to the last point, win or lose. An exciting and difficult thing about tennis is that, unlike sports where the clock can run out to end a game, a match isn't over until someone wins the final point. What this means is that, no matter how far you are behind, you're never completely out of it and the match isn't lost until your opponent wins the last point. Of course, this also means that, no matter how far ahead you are, your opponent is never out of it either.

As with prime start and prime process, your ability to have a prime finish is determined by your focus and your intensity. The hardest part of a match is closing it out. It's common for players, when they're serving for the match, to either become very nervous because they can't believe they're actually going to win, or experience a total letdown in their intensity because they've already mentally left the court. Both of these occurrences are caused by the same thing: a shift from a process focus to an outcome focus. Which response you have will depend on your confidence in your tennis and your experience with winning.

As soon as you start focusing on winning the match, several possible scenarios may occur. By realizing that you can win the match, many thoughts and emotions are triggered about winning. Perhaps you have not won that much, so you really can't believe that you might win the match. Or deep down you aren't sure you deserve to win. These thoughts will usually provoke doubt and anxiety which will, in turn, cause you to become cautious and tentative. When this happens, you have a shift from "I can win this match" to "I hope my opponent loses this match for me." You no longer have control of the match or over whether you will win or lose it. Your only hope is that your opponent has already lost mentally and doesn't put up a fight.

If you have confidence in your game and you have won regularly before, other thoughts and emotions will arise. The most common is: "I have this match won." In a sense, you are mentally leaving the court and picking up your trophy. There is just one minor problem; the match isn't over yet and you haven't won. You are no longer focusing on those things that enabled you to get to this point in the match where you can win. The prime intensity that allowed you to be in a position to win the match is no longer present, so you are physically incapable of maintaining your level of play.

The solution for both of the scenarios is simple: maintain your process focus and your prime intensity. If you have been in this situation before, you can almost be assured that one of these two responses will occur. You can plan for them and be prepared to take the necessary steps to combat these changes when they arise.

If you're losing the match, your greatest challenge is to not give up and to keep fighting. Knowing that your opponent is probably going to experience one of the above reactions should give you hope that you're not out of the match. Most players you compete against will see their games decline toward the end for these reasons. With this knowledge, you should gain renewed motivation to stay in the match and increased confidence that you still have a chance.

With this reinvigoration, your goal is to stay with a process focus, move closer to you prime intensity, and figure out if you need to make any changes to your game to take advantage of this opportunity. Understand that these efforts will not guarantee that you will come back and win. Your opponent may simply be too tough or you might not have the game to win this time. However, your efforts will certainly raise your game, enable you to put up a good fight to the end so your opponent has to earn the victory, and ensure that you have a prime finish.

"No. 1 is being mentally consistent."

Chris Evert

Chapter 12
Playing in Prime Time: Lessons from the Pros

Prime Time is what playing tennis is all about. It's the reason why you work so hard on all aspects of your game. Prime Time is the reason you're reading this book. The goal of *Prime Tennis* is for you to play your best in Prime Time.

Prime Time refers to match situations that really matter. The points that can turn a match toward you or against you. Prime Time can be coming back from 0-40 in the second game and breaking your opponent's spirit early. Prime Time can be having to hold serve to stay in the match when you're down a set and 4-5. It can be when you are in a final set tiebreak of a two-and-a-half hour match and you're exhausted.

Prime Time is that moment that defines you as a tennis player. It shows you and others how skilled you are, how well conditioned you are, and, most importantly, how strong you are mentally. This book has been directed toward you achieving Prime Tennis and being able to use it in Prime Time.

This notion of Prime Time emerged from my work with one young player who was making a difficult, though successful, transition from high-level junior tennis to the professional ranks. What became clear to both of us was that the professional game holds little resemblance to the junior game. The pros don't just do things better, they do things differently. These lessons that we learned together helped this player overcome the challenges of professional tennis and attain a high WTA ranking. They also showed me things that players at all levels could use to raise their games and achieve their highest level of tennis success, whether that is defeating their best friend for the first time, winning the club tournament, or earning the coveted gold ball for winning a USTA national championship. These lessons are divided into three categories: match, tactical, and mental.

"The simplest definition of a champion is the one with self-awareness closest to reality and seems able to execute best under pressure."

Billie Jean King

Match Lessons

1. *Play your game as well as you can.* Your game may not be the best it can be. You may not be playing that well. Whatever game you bring to the court, play it to the best of your ability. An important lesson I learned from working with pros is that you can't always play at 100%. Imagine the life of a touring pro. They play up to 30 tournaments a year. They travel constantly, sometimes going from one side of the world to the other and having to play the next day. There is simply no way they can be totally on top of their game for every match.

Many times, players walk onto the court and just don't feel very good, and know they're not going to play well. Because they're not going to play at 100%, they, in essence, throw in the towel before the match even begins. They think, "If I'm not feeling good, there's no way I can play well and win the match. So why even try."

However, as I said previously, you don't have to play great tennis to win matches. You only need to play better than your opponent. So, to increase the likelihood of that happening, you must learn to play your best with what you have on that given day. For example, if you're only at 80%, play at the full 80%. That may still be enough for you to win.

2. *KISS*. Tennis is really a simple game. Whoever gets the ball in the court last wins the point. Yet, players can make tennis complicated by trying to do too many things. A rule to follow is the KISS principle. Most players know the KISS principle as "keep it simple stupid," but I don't believe that one. I believe players should "keep it simple SMART!"

My KISS principle means that you should choose a few basic things you want to do in a match and stick to them. When things aren't going well, there can be a tendency to think too much and try to find some complex solution to the problem. This approach usually just clouds the situation and makes it worse.

Your goal should be to focus on a few things and do them to the best of your ability. If you look at the top players, they don't have complicated games. Each pro does a few things well and has one or two weapons on which they rely. Agassi has his return of serve. Hingis has her tactics and footwork. Venus Williams has her big serve and forehand. If they don't work in a match, you know you need to work on them more in practice. In a match, though, the chances of them working are much greater than if you make a few small changes and try not to do too many things.

3. *Have a game plan.* Playing a match without a plan is like an army going to battle without a strategy to defeat the enemy. Firepower, that is to say ability, is not always enough to overcome an opponent. A well-conceived plan and superior tactics can often overcome a more skilled player.

You have two goals in devising a game plan: maximize your strengths and exploit your opponent's weaknesses.

Before a match, decide on a few basic tactics that you do well and that you will use. The most important contributor should be what kind of game you have. It would make little sense to design a game plan that you're not technically capable of executing. A game plan should emphasize your strengths and minimize your weaknesses. For example, if your forehand is your best weapon and your backhand is weak, a strategy of hitting deep to your opponent's backhand will give you the opportunity to run around your forehand. It also opens up the court so you can use your big forehand to hit winners down the line from the ad court.

The second thing to consider in developing a game plan is your opponent's strengths and weaknesses. This input should be secondary to your game because you wouldn't want to create a game plan based on your opponent's weaknesses that you don't have the ability to execute. You may also not know anything about how your opponent plays. An ideal game plan is one that utilizes your strengths and neutralizes your opponent's strengths. This strategy provides the opportunity to gain control of the match by emphasizing what you do best and they do worst.

You also want to devise a backup plan in case Plan A doesn't work. If you recall my law of insanity, doing the same thing and expecting different results, you have to recognize when a game plan isn't working and isn't going to work. Yet, it's difficult to come up with another plan in the heat of a match. I recommend that you have a Plan B prepared before the match. Plan B should have the same goals as Plan A of maximizing your strengths and neutralizing your opponent's weaknesses, but offer another way to accomplish the goal. For example, Plan A may have been to exploit your opponent's slow foot speed by hitting short and giving her drop shots, but early in the match you find that when she gets to the short balls she's able to use her strong net game to win a lot of points. Plan B could be to achieve the same goal by hitting to alternate sides of the court and with more angles.

Having a Plan A and Plan B provides several benefits. Foremost, you have a "method to your madness" on the court. You're not just going out there and hoping to play well and win. Rather, you have a plan designed to enable you to play your best and maximize your chances of winning that will guide you through the match. Having a game plan will also boost your confidence because you have a way that you believe will allow you to play your best and win.

4. Expect it to be hard. This is one of the toughest lessons for young pros. As juniors, in the early rounds of tournaments, there are always easy matches. Scores of 6-0,-6-2 are commonplace. Not in the pros. Every match is hard. Every match is one they could lose because their opponents are just as good, just as competitive, and just as hungry to win.

Tennis should be difficult. That is what makes it so much fun and rewarding. If you play against someone whom you are considerably better than and you win, how do you feel? Not much sense of accomplishment and satisfaction, is there? Matches are supposed to be hard. They should be physically demanding. Matches should test your technical and tactical capabilities. They should show you what you are made of mentally and emotionally. That is why you compete. This is even more true when you play in Prime Time.

If you expect it to be hard, then there will be no surprises. If you fall behind, well, that is part of the game. If you choke, well, that happens. If you fight as hard as you can and still lose, well, you can still feel good for having given your best effort. If you expect it to be hard, you will prepare yourself physically and mentally for the demands of the match. When the match proves that you were right, it is tough, then you'll respond well and play your best tennis.

5. Win the mental game. As I alluded to in the preface, when you walk onto the court, you play two games. First, you play your opponent in the tennis game. Second, you play yourself in the mental game. Your opponent has a similar situation. Given fairly equal ability, whoever wins the mental game will win the match.

There are several keys to winning the mental game. Most importantly, you have to be your best ally rather than your worst enemy. If your opponent is against you and you are against you, you don't have a chance. Another key is to never give up. Remember what happens when you give up; you automatically lose. As long as you stay motivated and keep fighting no matter how you're playing or what the score is, you will always have a chance. Two essential mental skills are to maintain prime focus and intensity throughout the match. Without these two Prime Tennis skills, you will not be mentally or physically capable of playing your best. This entire book is designed to help you win the mental game.

> *"She used to get down on herself when she missed balls, and then she'd lose a couple of games because she was down. But she doesn't do it anymore. She understands that when you play a big, aggressive game, you're going to be missing balls sometimes. You have to stick with your game plan...and go for your shots."*
>
> Coach Robert Van't Hof of
> Lindsay Davenport

Tactical Lessons

1. *Get your first serve in.* One of the most significant predictors of who wins matches is first-serve percentage. This is because a first serve usually enables the server to control the point. Regardless of the actual speed of a first serve, returners' typical mindset is that it will be more difficult to return, so their goal is to just get the ball back in play. With a less aggressive return, the server is then able to dictate the point. Whoever dictates the point will usually win the point. It also takes pres-

sure off the server because there are fewer chances of double faulting when faced with a second serve.

I so often see my law of insanity at work with first serves. Players keep missing their first serves, but they don't do anything to change it. They keep trying to hit that first serve the same way in hopes that it will magically come around. Players are so committed to going for the big first serve that they don't consider modifying the serve so that it will go in.

When your first serve isn't working, it's best to take a little off it and get it in before going back to a big first serve. Remember that you still have the psychological first-serve advantage because your opponent doesn't know that you're hitting it at 75%. Even when you've done it a few times, your opponent doesn't know if you're going for a big serve on the next point. So your opponent will continue to focus on just returning the ball. Always follow this simple rule: it is better to get in a 75% first serve than to miss a 100% first serve.

2. *Grind out points.* It's natural to feel pressure and anxiety when you're playing in Prime Time. A common reaction to anxiety is to rush points and to end them quickly. This is a mistake. It will usually lead to unforced errors because you're trying to hit shots that you're not in a position to hit successfully. When you rush to end points, you're also communicating to your opponent that you want to get the point over with quickly and don't really want to be out there at all.

Patience on big points is essential. You should make it a rule not to go for first ball winners (unless, of course, your opponent hands you a shot you can put away). Instead, set up the point using a strategy that has worked earlier in the match. Look for high-percentage opportunities to win the point. This willingness to grind out points at critical stages of the match communicates to your opponent that you're willing to stay out there as long as it takes to defeat them.

3. *Be aggressive.* Another common response to Prime Time is to become tentative. By being cautious, players believe that they're playing high-percentage tennis because their goal is to simply get the ball back.

This is also a mistake because tentativeness usually translates into muscle tension, shortened strokes, and less power and depth. This uncertainty results in weak shots of which your opponent can then take advantage.

Being patient does not mean being tentative. It's important that when you get into Prime Time you continue to play aggressively. Being aggressive does not mean trying to hit winners on every shot or coming to the net behind every short ball. It means having an attitude that you're going to go for your shots and dictate the point. Whatever kind of shot you're going to hit, you hit it with authority and conviction.

You should also be willing to take chances periodically during a match. If you see an opening to go for a big shot, even if it is risky, go for it. This aggressiveness sends a powerful message to your opponent that you are confident and will take chances and not play it safe to win the match. It will also encourage you to not hold back. Such risks should be taken, however, when you can afford to lose a point if the risk fails

4. *Give yourself a margin for error.* In Prime Time, there can be a pressure to have to hit the perfect shot to win the point. Many players believe that only by hitting a shot on the line or in the corner can they win the point. The danger though is that there is no such thing as the perfect shot and when you try to "paint the lines," you end up giving yourself no room for error.

Even the best pros in the world do not have the ability to place the ball on a dime every time. Rather, they're good at hitting the ball consistently to a target area of, say, three or four feet around. They've also learned that they don't have to hit the perfect shot to win the point.

Particularly in Prime Time, you want to give yourself a margin for error, so even if you don't hit the ball exactly where you want, it will still go in the court and it will still be a good shot. A reasonable rule of thumb is to aim three feet from the sidelines or baseline. This larger target area will enable you to hit a shot that will be aggressive, yet will also be a high-percentage shot.

5. *Take advantage of weak shots.* What separates the best pros from those ranked below them is their ability to take advantage of weak shots. Of all

the tactical lessons that I learned while working with pros, this may have been the most important. The top pros jump all over an opponent's weak return without hesitation. In fact, this ability is deeply ingrained in their tactical psyches. They not only attack weak shots when they arise, but they're looking for them with every shot from their opponent. Moreover, they set up points with the expectation that one of their shots will lead to a weak shot worth taking advantage of.

The first step in developing this skill is knowing what weak shots are. Any shot that lacks pace, that sits up high, or lands within four feet of the service line may be considered a weak shot. These shots are ones that you can step into, use your forward momentum, and hit aggressively. This recognition process is not always easy because it has to occur in the middle of a point in which there are a lot of other things going on. A good technique for becoming more aware of weak shots is to remind yourself of this focus before a point and to say "weak" whenever one arises. In time, this recognition occur without conscious thought.

Next, you have to learn to react to them. This is the most difficult part of developing this ability. If you're not by experience an aggressive player, you may find that you recognize the weak shot too late and miss out on jumping on the shot. Again, you must remind yourself before a point that your goal is to recognize and respond to a weak shot. Then, when you're in the point, maintain your focus on weak shots. It will at first be uncomfortable if it's not a natural part of your game. With practice and seeing the great results of taking advantage of weak shots, you'll slowly ingrain the skill until it becomes a natural part of your tactical psyche and playing repertoire.

"I think consistency, waiting for the right ball, not getting impatient and making errors is the main difference in my game."

Lindsay Davenport

Mental Lessons

1. *Believe in your game.* As Chapter Four suggests, developing confidence in your game is one of the biggest challenges you face. Except for the very best pros, many players don't have that deeply ingrained belief in their game. I see this often early in matches. For example, a serve-and-volley player loses his first four trips to the net. Because he doesn't have complete confidence in his net game, he decides to stay on the baseline, even though there is ample evidence from the past that a baseline game won't work for him.

This confidence in their game is an essential quality that separates the great players from the good ones. Through experience and success, they gain such trust in their shots that even when a shot isn't working for them, they don't abandon it. Rather, they know that if they just keep hitting the shot, it will come around.

It's a mistake for the player in the last example to change his game just because it doesn't work right away. Instead, this player should keep serving and volleying. A lesson you can take from the pros is to believe in your game and know that it will, in time, enable you to play your best and win the match.

This belief will also serve you well in Prime Time. Imagine hitting a down-the-line forehand. You have probably hit thousands of them successfully. Yet, the essential question is, Can you hit that forehand at match point in the most important match of your life against the most difficult opponent you have ever faced? A lesson you can learn from the pros is to develop such a belief in your game that you truly know that you can hit any shot when you absolutely need to. This belief in your game gives you the confidence to go for big shots in Prime Time.

2. *Be ready for every point.* One of the first lessons young pros learn when they join the tour is that there are no free points. Every point is an opportunity to play well or play poorly. The type of point that is played will depends largely on how prepared players are to play every point.

This is important for young pros and their opponents. Young pros can expect that their more experienced opponents will make them work every step of the way. They must also be sure not to give easy points away. Loose points at critical stages of a match can mean the difference between who wins and who loses.

A lesson you can learn from the pros is to take your time and be sure that you are physically, technically, tactically, and mentally ready for every point. This practice serves several purposes. It enables you to recover physically and mentally from the last point. You can focus on the present and the process which will enable you to be more prepared for the next point. It also enables you to reduce your intensity which can be expected to rise, especially if the next point is an important one. By taking extra time, you can also develop a plan of how you want to play the next point.

Most importantly, your goal is to ensure that when you serve or receive, you are totally prepared to play your best. Only by being completely ready for every point will you be able to play well consistently and achieve Prime Tennis.

3. *Expect to be nervous in Prime Time*. Prime Time means the match you are playing matters. The match may be the finals of a big tournament or you may be in a third-set tiebreak. You may start to feel nervous because it's an important point in the match. This anxiety makes you uncomfortable, which raises doubts in your mind, causes you to feel negative emotions, and, because of all of these, you become more nervous. As a result, the quality of your game declines and you lose the match.

This reaction is common among players of all levels of ability. It is also one of the most harmful to Prime Tennis. Much of this book is directed toward helping you achieve prime intensity and not experience anxiety under pressure. The reality is, though, getting nervous before important matches and in big points is normal and natural. It happens to club players and it happens to the best players in the world.

One way to partially alleviate the negative effects of this nervousness is to expect be to nervous in Prime Time. If you anticipate experiencing some anxiety, when it arises, your reaction will be, "This is normal. I knew I would get a little nervous. No big deal," instead of "Oh no. I can't believe I'm getting nervous now. How can I play well feeling this way?"

Anxiety can also be interpreted in different ways producing very different reactions. If you view anxiety as negative and threatening, it will clearly hurt your game. If you see it, instead, as an indication that you're getting yourself prepared for the big match or a big point, that the feeling is not anxiety, but rather getting psyched up, then you will see it much more positively. With a more positive perspective on the added intensity, it will be less likely to produce negative thoughts and emotions, and, as a result, it will have a less harmful effect on your game.

Another important realization is that whatever you're feeling, your opponent is probably feeling the same doubts, anxiety, and emotions. Even if they look cool, calm, and collected on the outside, the chances are they're equally as nervous on the inside. This perspective offers even more support for the need to win the mental game. Given fairly equal ability, the player who wins the mental game is most likely going to win the match.

4. *Recover from errors quickly.* I If you recall, Prime Tennis is based on the notion that you can play at a consistently high level under challenging conditions. However, playing consistently does not mean that you will not make errors or experience declines in your level of play. One of the things that makes the world's best players so good is not that they don't make mistakes, but rather how quickly they recover from them. Matches are often won or lost based on which player can recover from their mistakes most quickly.

It's not uncommon for players to take up to several games to recover from a bad shot or a poorly played game. This occurs because they lose confidence, focus, and intensity, and they become frustrated, angry, or depressed due to of their poor play. It can take a while for them to get their head and their game together again and get back into the match.

Unfortunately, by the time they recover mentally and raise their game to its previous level, the match may be lost.

Recovering from mistakes quickly begins with a forgiving attitude in which you accept that you will make errors and you understand that negative thoughts and emotions, and poor focus and intensity will cause you to play worse. Accepting mistakes as part of tennis will make it easier for you to let go of the mistakes and poor play.

With the negative impact of mistakes reduced, you can then direct your attention to getting yourself back mentally and emotionally. This process begins with maintaining your confidence with positive thinking and body language. You can then redirect your focus onto the process and the present, in other words, what you need to do now to improve your game. You can also check and adjust your intensity to ensure your body is prepared to play at its prime level.

Having dealt with the mental and emotional aspects of mistakes, you can then directly address the cause of your poor play. You're going to miss shots with some regularity; a long first serve, a down-the-line forehand in the alley, a volley into the net. If a pattern starts to emerge in which you miss, for example, three first serves in a row, you should recognize that you have a problem that needs to be addressed. You can then identify the problem and find a solution. The problem might be technical or tactical. To solve the problem, you will need to make an adjustment in your game and focus on the solution in subsequent points.

5. *Accept the challenge.* The biggest obstacle to playing great tennis is fear. Fear produces in players a cautious attitude and a tentative game. On a practical level, this means that their main goal is to just get the ball back over the net. Players don't go for big serves when they need to, they don't hit out on shots, and they don't go for a winner when the opening presents itself.

There are few things more unsatisfying than going down with a whimper, not a bang. Players usually feel terrible when they play scared and they always regret having played such a careful game. This style of play simply won't work because for every shot that a player hits in fear and just tries to get back, their opponent is ready to fire back with full force.

Accepting the challenge does not mean trying to hit winners every shot. It does not mean serving and volleying every point. It means that whatever game you are playing in a match, you give it everything you have. If you hit a topspin forehand, you put all of your energy into hitting as heavy a topspin as possible.

Before a match, accept the challenge to play with courage and the willingness to risk in order to achieve Prime Tennis. Resolve to play your game to your fullest ability. Commit to doing everything you can to play your best and win the match. Accept that when you have this attitude, you still may not win. Understand that in Prime Time you can't always control whether you win or lose, but you can control the effort you put in, how hard you fight, and how well you play. If you do that, then you're much more likely to achieve Prime Tennis and, win or lose, you will feel good about how you played.

> *"You have to figure out a way to win. It's who's got the most guts, who's the better player in the end, and who's willing to lay it on the line for however long it takes."*
>
> Jim Courier

Section V

Prime Tennis Plan

Chapter 13
Prime Tennis Goal Setting

Goal setting is essential to being the best tennis player you can be. Motivation is not enough to be your best. Motivation without goals is like knowing where you want to go without knowing how to get there. Goals act as the road map to your desired destination. Goals increase your commitment and motivation and provide deliberate steps toward your tennis aspirations.

A Prime Tennis goal-setting program begins with a vision of where you want to go and what you want to do in your tennis. It also provides a clear why, what, where, and how for your efforts in striving for Prime Tennis. The Prime Tennis Goal Formula (see below) illustrates the important role that goals play in becoming a better tennis player.

PRIME TENNIS GOAL FORMULA

Motivation + Goals = PROGRESS

Types of Goals

There are five types of goals that you want to set in your Prime Tennis goal-setting program. *Long-term* goals represent what you ultimately want to achieve in your tennis such as to win the club championship, receive a tennis scholarship, or play professional tennis. *Yearly* goals indicate what you want to achieve in the next 12 months, for example, to attain a certain ranking or qualify for a particular tournament. *Competitive* goals specify how you want to perform in matches and tournaments you'll be playing in during the coming year. *Training* goals represent what you need to do in your physical, technical, tactical, and mental training to achieve your tournament goals. *Lifestyle* goals indicate what you need to do in your general lifestyle to reach your goals such as sleep, diet, work or school, and relationships.

Lower goals should support and lead progressively to the higher goals. For example, your lifestyle goals should help you accomplish your training goals which, in turn, should lead to your competitive goals, which should enable you to reach your yearly goals which finally should allow you to achieve your long-term goals.

> *"Unless you're really dedicated to a goal, there's no point in doing it."*

> World skiing gold medallist
> Hilary Lindh

Goal Guidelines

The effectiveness of a Prime Tennis goal-setting program depends on whether you understand what kinds of goals to set and how to use them to enhance your motivation and direction. There are five goal guidelines you should follow to get the most out of your goal setting.

1. *Goals should be challenging, but realistic and attainable.* You should set goals that can be reached, but only with time and effort. If you set goals that are too easy, you'll reach them with little effort, so they do little for your motivation. If you set goals that are too difficult, you won't be able to achieve them no matter how hard you try. This wouldn't help your motivation either since there would be little point in expending effort toward a goal you know you can't reach.

2. *Goals should be specific and concrete.* It's not sufficient to set a goal such as "I want to improve my serve." Goals should be clearly stated and measurable. For example, "I want to increase my first-serve percentage by 10%." This goal indicates the precise area to be worked on and the specific amount of improvement aimed for.

3. *Focus on degree of, rather than absolute, goal attainment.* An inevitable part of goal setting is that you won't reach all of your goals because it's not possible to accurately judge what is realistic for all goals. If you're only concerned with whether you reach a goal, you may perceive yourself as a failure if you're unable to do so. This response will invariably reduce rather than bolster your motivation. You should be more concerned with how much of the goal you achieve (degree of attainment) rather than whether or not you fully reach the goal (absolute attainment). Though you won't attain all of your goals, you will almost always improve toward a goal. With this perspective, if you don't reach a goal, but still improve 50% over the previous level, you're more likely to view yourself as having been successful in achieving the goal.

4. *Goal setting is a dynamic and fluid process.* Goal setting is a process that never ends. When one goal is achieved, you should set another goal that is higher or in a different direction to continually allow yourself to improve. You should review your goals regularly, compare them to actual progress, and adjust them as needed. Because you won't be able to set goals with perfect accuracy, you must be open to making changes as needed. For example, goals that you reach more easily than expected should be immediately

reset to a higher level. Conversely, if you set goals that were too difficult to achieve, you should modify them to a more realistic level.

5. *Prepare a written contract.* Research suggests that goal setting is most effective when it's prepared as a written contract comprised of explicit statements of your goals and the specific way you will achieve them. This approach clearly identifies your goals and holds you accountable for the fulfillment of the contract. You can complete a goal-setting contract, sign it, and give copies to your coach and others. To ensure that you continue to follow the contract, you can meet periodically with your coach to review your goals.

6. *Get regular feedback.* One of the most important contributors to the effectiveness of a Prime Tennis goal-setting program is consistent feedback. You should get regular feedback about how you're doing in pursuing your goals. This information can come from coaches, video analysis, physical testing, or with Prime Tennis Profiling. Consistent feedback that you're reaching your goals reinforces your motivation by showing you that your efforts are resulting in progress.

Using the Prime Tennis Goal Setting form (see page 181), write down your goals following the goal guidelines I just described. If you're uncertain of what your goals should be, ask your coach, your trainer, or others who know what you're working on.

> *"The resources of the human body and soul are enormous and beyond our present knowledge and expectations. We go part of the way to consciously tapping these resources by having goals that we want desperately."*

> Olympic track & field champion Herb Elliot

PRIME TENNIS GOAL SETTING

Directions: In the space below, indicate your Long-term, Yearly, and Competitive goals.

Long-Team (ultimate tennis dream):

Yearly (tournament and ranking goals for the year):

Competitive (goals for specific matches and tournaments):

PRIME TENNIS GOAL SETTING (cont.)

Directions: In the space below, set your Training and Lifestyle goals that will enable you to achieve your Competitive, Yearly, and Long-term goals. Also, under Method, indicate specifically how you will reach your Training and Lifestyle goals. Examples have been provided in *italics* for each type of goal.

Training (goals for all aspects of preparation):

Technical (*strokes, footwork, tactics*)

1.
   Method:

2.
   Method:

3.
   Method:

Physical (*strength, stamina, agility*)

1.
   Method:

2.
   Method:

3.
   Method:

PRIME TENNIS GOAL SETTING (cont.)

Mental (*motivation, confidence, intensity, focus, emotions*)

1.

Method:

2.

Method:

3.

Method:

Lifestyle (sleep, diet, work/school, relationships):

1.

Method:

2.

Method:

3.

Method:

Chapter 14

Prime Tennis Program

You now know what your goals are. The aim of the Prime Tennis program is to help you achieve these goals in the most efficient and organized way possible. You can develop your own individualized Prime Tennis program by following three steps: design, implementation, and maintenance.

Design

The first thing you must do in the *design* phase of developing your Prime Tennis program is to identify your most crucial mental needs. You can use the results from your Prime Tennis profile to help you specify what mental areas you need to work on most. You'll also have different areas you need to work on in different tennis settings. For example, focus might be most important when you're training, developing your tennis imagery skills may be most necessary off-court, and controlling your intensity may be most critical when you're playing matches. Using the Prime Tennis

Identification form (see page 187), list the mental areas that you want to focus on in training, off-court, and in matches.

The next thing you need to do in designing your Prime Tennis program is to specify Prime Tennis techniques you will use to develop the mental areas you've just identified. It's not feasible to use every Prime Tennis technique for a certain area. For example, I described six strategies you could use to build your confidence. You should narrow those choices to two or three techniques that you like most. To do this, experiment with the different techniques for a few days and see which ones you're most comfortable with. Once again using the Prime Tennis Identification form, list the two or three techniques you've chosen. I recommend that tennis imagery be a regular part of your off-court Prime Tennis program because it offers so many benefits to every mental area.

The final part of the design phase is to organize your Prime Tennis program into a daily and weekly schedule. Just as you plan your physical and technical training, you want to specify when you will be doing your Prime Tennis training. The Typical Prime Tennis Program (see page 188) illustrates how you can organize Prime Tennis techniques into a cohesive program. Using the Prime Tennis Planner (see page 191), indicate when and where you will use Prime Tennis techniques you've specified in the Prime Tennis Identification form.

"We need to know where we are going, and how we plan to get there. Our dreams and aspirations must be translated into real and tangible goals, with priorities and a time frame. All of these should be in writing, so that it can be reviewed, updated, and revised as necessary."

Former NFL great
Merlin Olsen

PRIME TENNIS IDENTIFICATION

Directions: In the space below, indicate the mental areas on which you need to work in the different settings. Then, specify Prime Tennis techniques you will use to develop these areas.

Setting	Mental Area	Prime Tennis Techniques
Training		
1.		
2.		
3.		
Off-Court		
1.		
2.		
3.		
Matches		
1.		
2.		
3.		

TYPICAL PRIME TENNIS PROGRAM

Mental Need and Goal	Mental Technique	Place in Schedule
Increase Motivation	Goal setting	Before season; monthly
	Two daily questions	At start and end of day
Build Confidence	Tennis Player's Litany	At start and end of practice
	Thought-stopping	In training and matches
Intensity Control	Deep breathing	During practice and matches
	Active relaxation	At end of practice
	Tennis routines	Before matches; between points
Overall Performance	Tennis imagery	Three times per week before dinner

Implementation

The second phase of the Prime Tennis program is *implementation*. This is where you put into action the Prime Tennis program you've just designed. It's best that you begin your Prime Tennis program as far in advance of your primary competitive season as possible. There are several benefits to starting your Prime Tennis program early. It enables you to develop the most effective Prime Tennis program possible. An early start allows you to incorporate it fully into your overall training program. It lets you fine-tune the program to best suit your needs. Most importantly, it gives you the time to practice the skills and gain its benefits.

A concern that players often have is the time commitment required for a Prime Tennis program. Certainly, they are busy enough without introducing one more thing into their lives, no matter how important it is. Players can spend hours every day in their physical and technical training and there simply wouldn't be similar time to devote to their Prime Tennis program. Fortunately, Prime Tennis training doesn't require hours a day to gain its benefits. Most Prime Tennis training can be incorporated directly into a traditional on- and off-court training program. Only about 10-15 minutes a day extra is needed for outside Prime Tennis training such as relaxation and tennis imagery.

If you feel that all of the areas and techniques you've identified in your Prime Tennis program are too much to do, then start small. Select half the techniques you've specified and work on those. You'll find that Prime Tennis training is not only not time consuming or overwhelming, but rather it is an enjoyable addition to your current training program and a nice break from your usual routine. You'll also find that you pick up Prime

Tennis techniques quickly and you'll get to the point where you do them without thinking about it.

> *"Tara [Lipinski] has her day structured so she's a giddy teenager between these hours and a really hard worker between these hours."*

Coach Richard Callaghan

PRIME TENNIS PLANNER

Time	Monday	Tuesday	Wednesday	Thursday	Friday	Saturday	Sunday
MORNING							
AFTERNOON							
EVENING							

Maintenance

The final phase of the Prime Tennis program is *maintenance*. The reality is that there is nô end to the use of Prime Tennis training. Just like physical conditioning and technical skills, mental skills will atrophy when they're not maintained through regular use. As I described in the Positive Change Formula, repetition is essential for you to maintain Prime Tennis. Fortunately, with practice, Prime Tennis skills become automatic, so you need less time and effort to retain them. For example, once you've developed your focus skills, it's easier to stay focused, so you don't have to pay as much attention to your focusing techniques.

Once you achieve Prime Tennis, you can adjust your Prime Tennis program to a lower, though still consistent, level of involvement. Also, as new problems arise, you can modify your Prime Tennis program to resolve them.

Postscript

To be motivated, confident, intense, and focused. To be an emotional master. To be your best ally on-court rather than your worst enemy. To play your best consistently under the most challenging conditions. These are the skills that Prime Tennis can help you develop.

Why is Prime Tennis so important to you that you would read this book and put such time and effort into your tennis? Your answer is a personal one. For some, it may be to have more fun playing tennis. For others, it may be to become the best tennis player they possibly can. For still others, it may be to win more matches.

I would like to believe, though, that the most compelling reason why you want to achieve Prime Tennis is to master what I have described as the most important and difficult game you play, in your tennis and in your life. That game is the *mental game*. If you can win the mental game and remove all of the obstacles that keep you from playing your best tennis and living your fullest life, then everything is possible.

By winning the mental game, you clear the path to happiness, fulfill-ment, and success in tennis and, yes, in life. I hope that, as you have read *Prime Tennis*, you've thought, "Hey, this could apply to my work" or "This relates to my relationships." Tennis, like life, is filled with challenges, struggles, excitement, setbacks, failures, and ultimately, mastery. Because to experience the "triumph of the mental game" is also to seize victory in the game of life.

Jim Taylor, Ph.D.
August, 2000

About the Author

Dr. Jim Taylor has been a consultant to USA Tennis Player Development and the Evert Tennis Academy. He is a regular speaker for the USTA and the USPTA. He has worked with many professional, collegiate, and junior-elite players. Dr. Taylor received his bachelor's degree from Middlebury College and earned his master's degree and Ph.D. in Psychology from the University of Colorado. He is a former Associate Professor and Director of Sport Psychology at Nova University in Ft. Lauderdale. A former U.S. top-20 ranked alpine ski racer, Dr. Taylor is also a USPTA-certified teaching professional, a 2nd degree black belt and certified instructor in karate, and a marathon runner. Dr. Taylor is the author of ten books, has published over 220 articles in magazines including *TENNIS, Sun Tennis, Inside Women's Tennis* and the magazines of the USPTA, and has given more than 300 workshops throughout North America and in Europe.

References

Apter, M. J. (1989). *Reversal theory: Motivation, emotion, and personality*. London: Routledge.

Butler, R. J., & Hardy, L. (1992). The performance profile: Theory and application. *The Sport Psychologist, 6*, 253-264.

Cautela, J. R., & Wisocki, P. A. (1977). Thought-stoppage procedure: Description, application, and learning theory applications. *Psychological Records, 27*, 255-264.

Ericsson, K., & Charnes, N. (1994). Expert performance: Its structure and acquisition. *American Psychologist, 49*, 725-747.

Jacobson, E. (1930). *Progressive relaxation*. Chicago: University of Chicago.

Moran, A. (1996). The psychology of concentration in sport performers: A cognitive analysis. East Sussex, UK: Psychology.

Nideffer, R. M. (1981). *The ethics and practice of applied sport psychology*. Ithaca, NY: Mouvement.

Singer, R. N., Murphey, M., & Tennant, L. K. (Eds.). (1993). *Handbook of research on sport psychology.* New York: MacMillan.

Taylor, J. (1996). *The mental edge for tennis* (4th ed.). Denver, CO: Minuteman.

Van Raalte, J. L., & Brewer, B. W. (Eds.). (1996). *Exploring sport and exercise psychology.* Washington, DC: APA.

Williams, J. M. (Ed.). (1998). *Applied sport psychology: Personal growth to peak performance* (3rd ed.), (pp. 219-236). Palo Alto, CA Mayfield.